THE SACRED LIFE OF WORDS

A Guide for Christian Writers

MARK WORTHING

Published by Acorn Press
An imprint of Bible Society Australia
ACN 148 058 306 | Charity licence 19 000 528
GPO Box 4161
Sydney NSW 2001
Australia
www.acornpress.net.au | www.biblesociety.org.au

ISBN 978-0-647-53047-4

First published by Morning Star Publishing in 2020, ISBN 978-0-647-53048-1

A catalogue record for this work is available from the National Library of Australia

Cover and text design and layout by John Healy
Cover image: Caravaggio - *Saint Jerome Writing,* c1606 - digitally altered.

Contents

Writing Prose

Odds and Ends

Preface

This is a book about writing. It is a book about writing creatively. It is book for those wanting to learn the writer's craft. It is a book for those seeking to improve their craft. There are hundreds of books out there that do all of these things quite well. So why this book? How is it different from the others? I would like to believe it is better organised, easier to understand and more practical than those other books. The reality is that it is probably not. What is different about this book is that it approaches the topic of the writer's craft from a distinctively Christian perspective and takes its examples largely from the world of Christian literature and publishing.

This book has its origins in a course of lectures developed over several years of teaching creative writing at a Christian tertiary institution. Much of my own writing, both fiction and non-fiction, falls under the broad category of Christian literature, and my editorial experience has also been with religious presses. So it made sense to incorporate the special concerns of the Christian writer in a book that began as a simple introduction to the basic skills of creative writing. This book is especially written for those writing for a Christian market, as well as those seeking to write consciously as people of faith for the mainstream market. The basics of writing poetry and prose are covered, but the topics addressed also include faith writing, the influence of the literature of the Bible, writing biblical historical fiction, writing religious poetry and publishing within a Christian market.

Finally, this book is more than a 'how to' book of writing. It is a celebration of words and wordsmiths. It is a celebration of the gifts of writing and creativity. It is a celebration of the Creative Word, in whose image we are both made and re-made. It is a book about the sacred life of words and those who craft them.

INTRODUCTION:

Creativity, Writing and the Christian Context

> *'It is incredible that a row of black marks on white paper can stir us to anger, shake us with laughter, or cause tears to tremble on our eyelids. Such is the power of written words.'*
>
> – Colin Thiele[1]

What is creative writing?

All writing is creative. Anytime we put pen to paper, or fingers to the keyboard, we are creating a new piece of written communication, whether it be a memo, minutes of a meeting, academic report, letter to a friend or the beginning of that long-anticipated novel. But when we speak of creative writing we usually have in mind particular kinds of writing, namely poetry and prose fiction. These are the forms of writing people read primarily for enjoyment. The exact dividing lines, however, may be blurred. Where, for instance, is the boundary between well-researched historical fiction and the creative re-telling of history? And what of so-called creative non-fiction?

Poetry is always considered creative writing – even the epic portrayals of historical events. If we write a romantic letter or tell of an historical event and put our words into verse, we have chosen to craft our words in a form that is aesthetically pleasing rather than a form that provides the most straightforward way of conveying information.

In the case of prose it is not the form but rather the subject matter that places a piece within the category of creative writing. Fiction, of whatever length and genre, is written to do more than simply communicate. Such writings are meant to amuse, arouse, entertain – perhaps even sadden or enrage – through the narration of a story or event, or the description of some person or thing that is, at least in part, the creation of the writer. Dr Seuss' *Cat in the Hat*, Tolkien's *Lord of the Rings* trilogy, the short

1 Colin Thiele, 'Poetry and the Magic of Words' in *Word Magic. Poetry as a Shared Adventure*, ed. Walter McVitty (Rozelle, NSW: PETA, 1985), 1.

stories of Edgar Allan Poe, the allegorical *Chronicles of Narnia* by C.S. Lewis and the fairy tales of Hans Christian Andersen are all examples of creative writing. The New Testament Gospels, C. S. Lewis' book *Miracles*, Gibbon's *Decline and Fall of the Roman Empire*, and this book on writing are not.

Creative writing in the Christian context

Whether such a thing as 'Creative Christian Writing' exists depends largely on how the terms are defined. Authors with a commitment to the Christian tradition do not write creatively any differently to the atheist, the Buddhist or the Muslim. The technique, the struggles, the overall process, are not distinct. It would be expected, however, that a Christian who is also a writer will be influenced by their faith commitment, at the very least at the subconscious level. In this sense, whatever style, genre or theme a writer takes up, the concept of a 'Christian writer' would refer to the personal faith of the writer and not the specific content of their writing. We might also understand 'Creative Christian Writing' as the writing of creative literature that is explicitly Christian in content. Bunyan's *Pilgrim's Progress*, Lewis' *The Chronicles of Narnia* and the whole explosion of Christian romance, sci-fi and historical fiction now appearing in Christian bookstores are examples of this category.

In this book, we will discuss the ways in which a commitment to Christ affects the themes and style of our writing, both consciously and subconsciously. This book is not specifically about how to write Christian fiction or Christian poetry, though those topics will also be covered. At its heart, it is simply a book about how to write. But it assumes that those who have a personal faith in Christ can and should integrate this commitment into their writing.

The creative impulse

As people created in God's image we should not be surprised at the human capacity for creativity and imagination. Every culture, ancient and modern, has had its storytellers. Elaborate epic tales were told around campfire and hearth, using mnemonic devices that eventually became incorporated into written poetry. As cultures developed written language, the oral storyteller became the writer. The oldest stories in most cultures are generally poetic in form and reflect the epic oral tales that were put down into writing. These include the *Epic of Gilgamesh* (Assyrian, 20th century BCE), The *Iliad* and *Odyssey* (Greek, 8th century BCE), Virgil's *Aenid* (Latin, 1st century BCE), *Beowulf* (Old English, 9th century), the *Shahnameh* (Persian, 11th century), *The Saga of Grittir* (Icelandic, 13th century) and the *Nibelungenlied* (German, 13th century).

Wherever people went and thrived, the impulse to create stories for entertainment and edification has been present. But from where does this desire to create and write come? From the Christian perspective we would answer that it is part of the manifestation of being made in the image of a creative God. The desire to create, whether in the visual or literary arts or some other form, and the ability to appreciate that which has been created (good painting, good cinema, good writing) is inherent in all human beings. For those at home in the world of written words, the desire to write creatively is simply part of who we are as people made in the image of God.

Writing as a calling

For the Christian author, writing should be viewed as a vocation, or calling – whether one is able to make a living at it or not. The question is not so much, 'Can I write?' but 'Should I write?' We are really asking: 'Is this what I am called to do?' There is no easy answer to this question with regard to writing any more than there is for any other type of vocation or service. If someone is looking for a divine revelation or some other unmistakable sign from God as to whether or not they should be a writer, they may end up waiting a long time. More often than not, it's the simple things we should be looking for. A former lecturer of mine once advised: 'If you are trying to work out whether God is calling you to a certain vocation, try to do something else. If you are happy doing anything else – or can imagine being happy doing anything else – then that's an important indicator.' The inverse is also true. As the Christian author Liz Curtis Higgs wrote: 'The surest sign that I am called to write is this: I am happiest when I am writing. The sense of rightness and satisfaction is overwhelming.'[2]

2 Cited in D. Elble, *Behind the Stories* (Minneapolis: Bethany House, 2002).

Writing Poetry

Chapter 1

Beginning with Poetry

> *'Poetry is the most ancient and the most natural form of literature. Prose fiction is a latecomer.'*
>
> – Gene Veith[1]

> *'The distinction between poets and prose writers is a vulgar error.'*
>
> – Percy Bysshe Shelley[2]

Poetry as the foundation of creative writing

Many writers assume that poetry is an advanced form of writing that should only be taken up, if at all, after much experience with prose forms. The reality, however, is that poetry is foundational. Both in terms of the history of literature and of human literacy, poetry comes first. The great epic stories such as the *Iliad* and the *Odyssey* that stand at the heart of all literate societies are all in poetic form.[3] So too, young children are exposed predominantly to poetry in their earliest experience with books. Dr Seuss is a children's poet whose work is usually either alliterated, metred, rhymed or all of the above. Nursery rhymes are just that. Read a few classic children's stories carefully and you will detect that many are actually poetic in form. While poetry may at some levels be more difficult to construct, it is much easier to remember. This is why oral storytellers used it, and why it is so successful in children's literature.

It makes sense, therefore, to begin a book on creative writing with poetry. Poetry is not only the older and more fundamental form of

1 Gene Veith, Jr. *Reading Between the Lines. A Christian Guide to Literature* (Wheaton, Ill. Crossway Books, 1990), 79.

2 Percy Bysshe Shelley, *A Defence of Poetry*, in H. Needham, ed. *Sidney An Apology for Poetry: Shelley. A Defence of Poetry* (London: Ginn and Company, n.d), 74.

3 And it is not only the classic early stories that were put in poetic form. Sir Philip Sidney observed in his Elizabethan era defence of poetry: 'So Thales, Empedocles, and Parmenides sang their natural philosophy in verses; so did Pythagoras and Phocylides their moral counsels; so did Tyrtaeus in war matters, and Solon in matters of policy.' *An Apology for Poetry*, ed. H. Needham (London: Ginn and Company, n.d), 3.

creative writing, but learning to read and write poetry teaches skills that every good writer of prose fiction should possess. Poetry teaches us to be attentive to words. It teaches us to be attuned to the alliterations, rhymes, rhythms, and metre of our language. It teaches us to not be satisfied with the first word that comes to mind, but to search for the word that conveys our intended meaning in the most aesthetically pleasing way.

Poetry and language

Every language has its own forms of poetic expression that are uniquely suited to it. Metre and rhyme work well in English, but not in many other languages. French, which is unstressed, tends to work with syllabic structures. Languages with heavy reliance on regular systems of endings, like Greek, find rhyme less effective because too many words rhyme. This is one reason why poetry is notoriously difficult to translate. The meaning is easy enough to transport from one language to another, but puns, innuendo, word play, homonyms, synonyms, alliterations and rhymes in most cases simply do not translate. And if we translate poetry from a tonal language into a stressed language, the meaning of the poem might be preserved, but the feel of the poem lost. Good poets seek out the unique features and qualities of the language in which they write. For those of us who write poetry in English it is especially important to know the history of the language.

English is a hybrid language. About half the key words we use every day are of Germanic origin, and the other half of Romance (Roman) origin. While every language picks up numerous loan words from other languages over time, two distinct languages blending together to form one new language is rare. From the fifth century onward, Germanic tribes migrated to England, pushing out or overwhelming the Celtic population. They brought with them a number of Old Germanic dialects that we now collectively refer to as Old English. If left alone, English today would have remained a very near kin of German and Dutch, and would have also been more closely related to the Nordic languages. But in 1066, French speaking Normans led by William the Conqueror successfully invaded England. They set themselves up as the nobility of the country, and French dominated official life for three hundred years. The Normans, however, had little interest in forcing the English peasantry to speak

French, so a bilingual system developed in which French was the official language of law and politics (and Latin of the church), while the common people continued to speak their Germanic dialects. Without wealthy and educated speakers of Old English, however, there was little literature produced, and no formal learning of the language. Soon, the Germanic grammar began to give way and prepositions increasingly did the work of case endings. Also, a growing number of French words (themselves evolved from Latin) were being adopted by the common people, and the French-speaking nobility were picking up numerous Old English words.

The result of the two language traditions existing side by side was the production of a wide range of synonyms (very useful for writers!). These also tend to reflect the cultural origins of the words. Words for body parts (elbow, hand, bone, head, neck, foot), common animals (cat, hound, wolf) and common professions (baker, smith, shoemaker), are Germanic. Words for legal and church affairs, the life of the court, professions requiring some specific education (professor, cleric, ambassador, courtier) all came from the French or Latin. The common people were the ones who raised the animals, therefore we have simple Germanic words like swine, cow and sheep. But when the meat of these animals is eaten (it was usually the wealthy French occupiers who could most afford this) they were give names such as pork, veal and mutton.

Germanic origin words tend to be simple, bold and more guttural. The Latin and French based words more complex, subtle and flowing. The different sounds reflect the different linguistic origins. This is important as the feel, sound and cultural associations of individual words are vital in poetry. A good poet must be aware of this vocabulary divide that still lies at the heart of the English Language, and must know when to employ which type of word.

The following are two poems I composed to illustrate the different texture and feel of the two different vocabulary groups. The first poem is constructed entirely of words with Germanic and Norse etymologies.

Wasser unser[4]

Come forth, rain
Flow through heaven's gate;
Blot sun with cloud
As ploughmen shout aloud:

Fill our streams with watery swills,
Turn clay to mud – whate'er it wills
Bring life from death, quick'ning earth
With newborn grass and rose-white blooms

That trim young apple shoots
At war again with oak and ash
For rights of leaf and trunk to drink their fill
From unseen roots, which have no other will.

The next poem is constructed primarily of key words with Latin or Greek etymologies.

Dulce et decorum est
pro sui cogitere[5]

Random reflections
on quantum simultaneity
and other partially cogitated
theorems of the mind,
stand sentinel
over elusive intellects;

---

4 A pun on "*Vater unser, der du im Himmel bist*" (Our Father, who are in heaven.) The opening words of the Lord's Prayer in German are also the name of the prayer.

5 A pun on the Latin line, "*Dulce et decorum est pro patria mori*," from Horace's Odes. (It is sweet and fitting to die for one's country). Wilfred Owen famously punned this ancient piece of pro-war propaganda in his WW1 poem 'Dulce et decorum est' describing a mustard gas attack. *Dulce et decorum est pro sue cogitere* means roughly, 'It is sweet and fitting to think for one's self.'

now connected via modem and remote
to uninhabited ether,
like galactic black holes
exploring the *creatio de novo*
of abandoned space and mind.

The sounds, feel and mood of the two poems are strikingly different. Much of this has to do with the vocabulary chosen. The astute wordsmith, especially the poet, will choose words carefully with an eye (and ear!) to their origins. Words from the same or similar family background usually sound better together. A predominance of words from one group or the other can set the tone of a poem.

Exercise Germanic versus Romance vocabulary

Write a short poem using primarily or even exclusively Germanic base words. Then do the same with Romance base words from French or Latin (feel free to include Greek base words in this lot as well). The latter poem will need to include some Germanic words such as English prepositions, pronouns, conjunctions and articles as these are all Germanic in origin.

Chapter 2:

Finding Inspiration in the Poetry of the Bible

'The artistic impulse is everywhere evident in biblical poetry... The poets who wrote the poetry of the Bible loved not only God and his truth but also poetry. They were interested in poetry as a craft.'

– Leland Ryken[1]

'It is probable that the poetry of Moses, Job, David, Solomon, and Isaiah has produced a great effect upon the mind of Jesus and his disciples.'

– Percy Bysshe Shelley[2]

Biblical Hebrew poetry

The ancient Hebrews made use of a traditional form of unrhymed poetry that is preserved in many parts of the Hebrew Bible.[3] Like all poetry, Hebrew poetry is built upon images, metaphors and similes. It says important things in the best and most beautiful way. Structurally, Hebrew poetry is distinctive. It is characterised by parallelism, a structural device in which the second line in a couplet says the same thing as the first line, but in a different way – or it parallels the first line in some other way. The Psalms are good examples of this type of poetry. Hebrew parallelism can occur in three different ways.

Firstly, and most common, is *synonymous* parallelism, in which the two halves of the verse make the same point or statement.

1 Leland Ryken, *Words of Delight. A Literary Introduction to the Bible*, 2nd ed. (Grand Rapids: Baker, 1992), 187.
2 Percy Bysshe Shelley, *A Defence of Poetry*, ed H. Needham, (London: Ginn and Company, n.d), 89.
3 For an excellent and readable study of the poetry of the Hebrew Bible, see Robert Alter, *The Art of Biblical Poetry* (New York: Basic Books, 1985).

Give ear to my words, O Lord;
Give heed to my sighing…

O Lord, in the morning you hear my voice:
In the morning I plead my case to you, and watch. (Psalm 5:1,3)

Secondly, is *antithetical* parallelism, in which the second line contradicts or contrasts with the content of the first line. This form of parallelism is fairly rare in the main poetical works of the Hebrew Bible, but occurs frequently in Proverbs.

Rash words are like sword thrusts,
But the tongue of the wise brings healing.

Truthful lips endure forever,
But a lying tongue lasts only a moment. (Proverbs 12:18f)

Finally, there are a number of couplets that do not fit into either of these categories. Yet the second line stands in some specific and distinctive relationship to the first, often qualifying or expanding upon it. These lines have generally been denoted as *synthetic* parallelism. This is essentially the 'everything else' category. Some good examples of so-called synthetic parallelism can be found in the first two stanzas of the great Hebrew alphabet poem, Psalm 119.

I will praise you with an upright heart,
When I learn your righteous ordinances. (conditional)

I will observe your statutes;
Do not utterly forsake me. (cause and effect)

How can young people keep their way pure?
By guarding it according to your word. (question and answer)

I have hidden your word in my heart
That I might not sin against you. (purpose)
(Psalm 119:7-9,11)

Hebrew poetry can also make use of other structures, such as the alphabet poem of Psalm 119, cited above. In this poem there are twenty-two stanzas (one for each letter of the Hebrew alphabet) of eight couplets each. The first word of each of the eight couplets in the first stanza all begin with the letter (א) *aleph*, the second with (ב) *beth*, and so on. Hebrew poetry also commonly displays chiastic structures in which the first and last couplets parallel each other in some way, again the second and penultimate couplets stand in parallel, and so on to the centre of the poem. Closely related to chiastic poetry is the concentric poem. Concentric structured poems have a couplet or line at the centre which has no parallel and which usually indicates the theme or key point of the poem. A classic example of a Hebrew poem with parallelisms and a concentric structure in found in Isaiah 43:1-7.

Can you find all the parallelisms as well as the concentric structure in the following poem? Try working from both ends of the poem, looking for key words and phrases, and match these to their parallels on the other side/half of the poem.

This now is what Yahweh says

He who created you, Jacob
He who formed you, Israel:
'Fear not, for I have redeemed you;
I have called you by name, you are mine
If you pass through the waters,
I am with you;
And if you pass through rivers,
They will not overwhelm you;
If you walk through fire
You will not be burned,
And if you walk through flames
They will not consume you.
For I am Yahweh your God

The Holy One of Israel, your saviour.
I give for your ransom Egypt,
Cush and Seba in exchange for you.
Because you are precious and honoured in my sight,
And I love you;
I will give people in exchange for you,
And nations in return for your life.
Fear not, for I am with you:
From the east I will bring your seed,
From the west I will gather you.
I will say to the north, 'Yield,'
And to the south, 'Do not hold back;
Bring my sons from afar,
And my daughters from the end of the earth,
All who are called by my name,
Whom I created for my glory,
Whom I formed and made."[4]

A structural outline of Isaiah 43:1-7 shows the poem to have four main points in the first half (indicated by A, B, C and D) and four points paralleling these (in reverse order, D', C', B' and A') in the second half. If this were all there were to the outline, the structure would be *chiastic* (named after the Greek letter Chi [X]). The appearance at the centre of the poem of a couplet which has no parallel or counterpart makes the structure *concentric* (sharing a common centre), and indicates the central point or theme of the poem.

4 Translation my own.

A God created/formed Israel

B God called God's people by name

Fear not

C Waters/rivers // fire/flame

Who God is … saviour

D Nations given in exchange for God's people

Focus → **E** **Because we are precious and God loves us (v. 4)**

D' People given in exchange for God's people

Fear not

C' East/west // north/south

Who God's people are … sons and daughters

B' God's people called by God's name

A' God created/formed the 'called' ones.

There is great intricacy and beauty in Hebrew poetry. Because so much of it is based on repetition, parallelism and structure, much of this beauty carries through in translation into other languages. Yet despite this, the form of Hebrew poetry has not exercised any significant influence on English poetry. This is due largely to two reasons. Firstly, the form of Hebrew poetry was not well understood or appreciated during the formative periods of classical English poetry. The structures of Hebrew poetry are obvious once spotted, and the first readers of these poems would have picked them up immediately upon reading or hearing them. Yet two centuries of modern biblical scholarship missed these structures almost entirely because we were not attuned to the rhythm and patterns of Hebrew poetry. Secondly, the forms did not suit the natural sounds and structure of English as well as did other forms. Nonetheless, parallelism can be used to good effect in English language poetry.

Exercise: Semitic symmetry

Write a short poem using parallelism. You may choose a theme echoing the psalms, or a very different, more modern theme. It is important that each couplet consists of lines that somehow parallel one another. To make it more interesting, follow that sense of symmetry or parallelism throughout the poem by adopting either a concentric or chiastic structure. Aim for 10-20 lines.

What follows is a poem in concentric structure. It deliberately reflects the style of Hebrew verse, while also having a traditional iambic metre (see chapter three) and simple a-a-b-b rhyme scheme, thus combining traditional Hebrew and English poetic forms. Note the suitability of both parallelism and chiastic structure for social and political critique. The centre couplet is set out on its own to show that it is shared by both halves of the poem. It is easy to see why so many of the Hebrew prophets turned to this form of poetry to express their words of warning.

Antipodean Arrivals

They landed on these southern shores in chains;
With antipodean gaols pre-built along the plains.
In rat-infested stinking ships they came;
In barques that scarcely stayed afloat in rain.
From Sheffield 'cross to Leeds they emptied gaols;
Cleaned out the streets from Belfast down to Wales.
With forc'ed labour they must bow the head:
Four years hard work for simply thieving bread.
First fleeters, wreathed, held up in honour now;
We fete unwilling pioneers somehow,

Deported nightmares landed on our shore.
They came with dreams of newfound life, and more;

These immigrants were not sent for by us;
Unwelcome queue jumpers we cannot trust.
In Baxter they must wait four years or more;
No work awaits them at our bolted door.
They've fled Sumatra, Timor and Iran;
Left Baghdad, Basra and Afghanistan.
They came in trawlers struggling just to float;
In rusting hulks they cross our ocean moat;
They landed free upon our fertile coasts;
Were carried off to Baxter by their hosts.

Poetry in the New Testament

While the poetic forms of the Hebrew Bible are nowadays quite well-known, the Greek New Testament also contains examples of poetry. For the most part these are found in songs that are quoted in the letters of St Paul. Some examples of these are the sacramental hymn of Titus 3:4-7, the meditative hymns of Romans 8:31-39 and Ephesians 1:3-14, the confessional hymns of 1 Timothy 6:11-16 and 2 Timothy 2:11-13, the Christological hymns of Colossians 1:15-20 and, most famously, the *Carmen Christi (*or *Song of Christ)* of Philippians 2:5-11,[5] and the eschatological hymn of 1 Thessalonians 1:9,10. While in English translation much of the poetic character of these songs is lost, in Greek the poetic form is unmistakeable. Like English, metre is often used (reflecting the likely origin of these poems as early Christian songs) and there are often basic chiming patterns – though these differ markedly from modern English rhymes.

The short eschatological hymn of 1Thessalonians 1:9, 10 − likely an excerpt from a longer song − provides a classic example of these poetic elements. Notice especially the use of pronouns (underlined in the Greek text) that are either repeated or occur in an order not typical of prose. Also, the first four lines all chime (with the second line an 'inverted rhyme'), as do the last four words of the final line. In order to better appreciate the structure of this Greek verse each line is given first in Greek, then in transliterated form, and finally in English translation.

Ἐπεστρέψατε προς **τόν** θε**όν** άπό **τϖν** είδώλ**ων**
*Epestrephate pros ton the**on** apo **ton** eidol**on***
You turned to God from idols

Δουλεύ**ειν** θε**ϖ** ζ**ϖ**ντι καί αληθι**νϖ**
*Douleu**ein** the**o** zo**n**ti kai alethi**on***
To serve God, living and true

---

5 A useful discussion of the literary features of this text that sheds light on the nature of the poetic sections of the New Testament is found in Ralph Martin, *Carmen Christi: Philippians 2:5-11 in Recent Interpretation and in the Setting of Early Christian Worship*, revised ed. (Grand Rapids: Eerdmans, 1983), 24-41.

Καί άναμέν**ειν** **τον** υί**όν** αύτόῦ έκ **των** ούραν**ϖν**,
*Kai anamen**ein** **ton** qui**on** autou ek **ton** ouran**on***
And wait for his Son from heaven,

ὅν ἤγειρεν έκ **τϖν** νεκ**ϖν**
*on ageiren ek **ton** nek**on***
Who was raised from the dead –

Ἰησο**ῦν** **τόν** ρυόμεν**ον** ήμας έκ **της** όργ**ης** **της** έρΧομεν**ης**.
*Ies**oun** **ton** ruomen**on** am**as** ek **tas** org**as** **tas** erkomen**as***
Jesus, who delivers us from the wrath to come.[6]

The New Testament poetic tradition is carried on perhaps most authentically in the sung poetry (hymns and songs) of the Christian community. Poetry was an established vehicle of biblical revelation, and has remained a vital part of Christian worship.

6 Translation my own.

Chapter 3

Keeping the Beat – The Importance of Metre

> *'You can write a poem and know nothing of metrics, just as you can play a piano and be unable to read music. But why choose ignorance?'*
>
> – John Whitworth[1]

Metre

Every language has its own poetic forms and devices. We have seen how two quite different poetic forms were employed in biblical Hebrew and New Testament Greek. English, with its unique history and sounds, has developed and often borrowed poetic devices particularly suited to it.

One of the most basic elements of traditional English poetry is metre. English is a stressed language, which means the alternating pattern of stressed and unstressed syllables can be used to create a regular rhythm that may be either somewhat hidden, or very obvious, depending on the particular metre used. In early English poetry, like *Beowulf*, these stresses were not patterned in the classical sense of Greek metre, but were regulated by having a set number of stressed syllables, often four, in each line. This, combined with the frequent use of alliteration (the repetition of initial word sounds), gave the poetry of the language a very strong and earthy rhythm.

Listen to the following lines from *Beowulf* and try to pick up the rhythm. Each line can be divided into two halves with two stressed words in each half. Keep in mind that alliteration is often used to highlight which words should be stressed.

So the company of men led a careless life,
all was well with them: until One began
to encompass evil, an enemy from hell.

1 John Whitworth, *Writing Poetry*, 2nd ed. (London: A and C Black, 2006), 71.

Grendel they called this cruel spirit,
the fell and fen his fastness was,
the march his haunt. This unhappy being
had long lived in the land of monsters
since the Creator cast them out
as kindred of Cain. For that killing of Abel
the eternal Lord took vengeance.
There was no joy of that feud: far from mankind
God drove him out for his deed of shame!
from Cain came down all kinds of misbegotten
– ogres and elves and evil shades–
as also the giants, who joined in long
wars with God. He gave them their reward.

This form of poetry continues into the early Middle-English period, and it is found in such poems as *Sir Gawain and the Green Knight*. Again, we find the standard four stresses per line, with usually at least three of the stressed words alliterated.

He rode far from his friends, a forsaken man,
Scaling many cliffs in country unknown.
At every bank or beach where the brave man crossed water,
He found a foe in front of him, except by a freak of chance,
And so foul and fierce a one that he was forced to fight.
So many marvels did the man meet in the mountains,
It would be too tedious to tell a tenth of them. (stanza 31)

An attempt to reclaim this early English use of metre was made in the late nineteenth century by the Jesuit priest Gerard Manly Hopkins. Hopkins meters his lines by placing the same number of stresses, usually four after the pattern of Old English, in each line. Similar to Old English, his stressed words often alliterate, making it easier and more natural to stress the right sounds. In lines where the stresses are not readily apparent, Hopkins placed accent marks over the stressed syllables. He called his technique 'sprung rhythm.' An excellent shorter example of this technique can be seen in his poem, *Inversnaid*. Notice also Hopkins' preference for words of Anglo-Saxon (Germanic) origin.

This darksome burn, horseback brown,
His rollrock highroad roaring down,
In coop and in comb the fleece of his foam
Flutes and low to the lake falls home.

A windpuff-bonnet of fáwn-fróth
Turns and twindles over the broth
Of a pool so pitchblack, fell-frówning,
It rounds and rounds Despair to drowning.

Degged with dew, dappled with dew
Are the groins of the braes that the brook treads through,
Wiry heathpacks, flitches of fern,
And the beadbonny ask that sits over the burn.

What would the world be, once bereft
Of wet and of wilderness? Let them be left,
O let them be left, wildness and wet;
Long live the weeds and the wilderness yet.[2]

Despite the strong tradition, the best-known of the Middle English poets, Geoffrey Chaucer, abandoned the Old English rhythms for iambic pentameter. This was a metre taken over from the Greek – via the French. The following description of the Knight's Squire from the prologue is a good example of this new style of English poetry.

There was a Yeoman with him at his side,
No other servant; so he chose to ride.
This Yeoman wore a coat and hood of green,
And peacock-feathered arrows, bright and keen
And neatly sheathed, hung at his belt the while
– For he could dress his gear in yeoman style,
His arrows never drooped their feathers low –
And in his hand he bore a mighty bow.

---

2 Gerard Manly Hopkins. *Poems and Prose*, ed. W. Gardner (New York: Penguin, 1985), 50f.

Most English poets followed Chaucer in adopting the metre of classical Greek and Latin poetry, which soon supplanted the more native metre. The most famous such metre is called the iambic. Iambic metre consists in 'feet' or sequences of two syllables: an unstressed followed by a stressed. The shortest lines in iambic would be those of only a single foot, that is, two syllables. The following is an example of iambic dimeter, laid out as monometer for effect.

Iambs
In Line

I am
in line
I am
supine
I am
not here
I am
not near
I am
divine
I am
in pine
I am
thus spread
I am
quite dead.

The following is an example of true iambic monometer.

The Hill

We filled
And tilled
The hill
With rocks
And stocks

To block
Undrained
Ordained
Spring rain
That sweeps
And heaps
The steep
With staged
And gauged
Rampage
That swills
And stills
Our hill.

All the various combinations of metre have Greek names and are derived from Greek antecedents. But while the standard metres used in English poetry are found already in Greek, the form and effect are very different. In Greek, 'feet' were measured by the repeated combinations of long and short syllables, whereas in English, there is a beat to the language which the poet is able to manipulate into regular combinations of stressed and unstressed syllables.

Types of classical metre which occur in English are shown below. The flat lines [-] indicate stressed syllables, and the upward curving lines [˘].unstressed syllables.

Iambic ˘ ¯ / ˘ ¯	By **nine** I'm **near**ly **done** with **hay**
Trochaic ¯ ˘ / ¯ ˘	**Will**iam **Yeats** is **laid** to **rest**
Anapestic ˘ ˘ ¯ / ˘ ˘ ¯	and the **peak** of the **mount**ain was **app**les
Dactylic ¯ ˘ ˘ / ¯ ˘ ˘	**Por**celain **dolls** never **dance** when we're **look**ing
Spondaic ¯ ¯ / ¯ ¯	**Earth**, **wind**, **fire**, **sea**
Amphibrachic ˘ ¯ ˘ / ˘ ¯ ˘	There **was** an old **la**dy from **Hahn**dorf

Iambic and trochaic are the most common and the easiest metres to detect. Anapestic and dactylic metres occur in English poetry but often go initially unnoticed. Spondaic metre is difficult to sustain and usually occurs over a limited number of words, often lists or other unusual grammatical constructions. A burst of spondaic metre can produce a good effect as a line within free verse or as a break within a poem of some other metre.

The metre pattern of English poetry is easier to understand when we recognise that iambic and trochaic are essentially the same pattern, as are anapestic and dactylic. The main differentiating feature is whether the line begins with a stressed or unstressed syllable. While true trochaic and dactylic lines should end with unstressed syllables, they often end with a stressed syllable for the sake of effect and the conventions of English rhyme. But they will always begin with a stressed syllable, in contrast to their more common iambic and anapaestic counterparts.

The other identifier placed on metered poetry concerns the number of feet per line. *Feet* indicates the number of times the pattern of stressed and unstressed syllables repeats itself in each line. The designation iambic pentameter, for instance, simply means that the poem is written in alternating unstressed and stressed syllables (iambic metre), and that this pattern repeats itself five times in in each line. The main possibilities in terms of number of feet per line are:

Monometer = one foot per line
Dimeter = two feet per line
Trimeter = three feet per line
Tetrameter = four feet per line
Pentameter = five feet per line
Hexameter = six feet per line
Heptameter = seven feet per line

Tennyson was a master of rhyme and metre. Neither the rhyme scheme nor metre is mistakable in the following untitled sonnet.

The pallid thunder-stricken sigh for gain,
Down an ideal stream they ever float,
And sailing on Pactolus in a boat,

Drown soul and sense, while wistfully they strain
Weak eyes upon the glistening sands that robe
The understream. The wise, could he behold
Cathedraled caverns of thick-ribbéd gold
And branching silvers of the central globe,
Would marvel from so beautiful a sight
How scorn and ruin, pain and hate could flow:
But Hatred in a gold cave sits below;
Pleached with her hair, in mail of argent light
Shot into gold, a snake her forehead clips,
And skins the colour from her trembling lips.[3]

In the following poems I have employed standard metre schemes. Notice the distinctive rhythms created by the use, respectively, of iambic pentameter and irregular dactylic hexameter. The metre of each poem fits the mood and theme of that particular poem. The steady monotonous iambic is indicative of the long hard days in the hayfield, whereas the more rhythmic and flowing dactylic is suited to the gaiety of the dancing figurines.

I Dream Hayfields

I walk to work across a field;
along a brown, dry, brittle row
of hay that just four days ago
stood grassy fresh against the yield.
And though the work seems never done,
I tread atop the heat-cracked clay
and toss the bails t'ward wagon tongue,
while marching on throughout the day
to rhythmic beat of old John Deere,
circling the field I'm sure we've done
already twice before this year.

---

3 Alfred Lord Tennyson. *The Poetical Works* (New York: Houghton, Mifflin and Company, n.d.), 412.

By time we've done a round or two
I've so much chaff stuck to my skin
that when I sweat I itch still worse
so that I could not hope begin
recount the times I thought to curse
the chaff stuck on my back, my hair;
inside my shoes, my socks and shirt.
My arms are hay-scratched everywhere,
from tossing bails up eight tier high.
My burdened back now aches with hurt
from burning toil, and I would cry,
had I the time or tears to spare.

By nine I'm nearly done with hay,
as evening steals away my sight.
But we still have one load to lay,
so search the barn in dimming light
to find above a startled cat
an overworked extension lamp.
With tit-for-tat, by ten at that,
we've cleared the bails from off the ramp.
Now eyelids hang like leaden shields
as I take leave to rest at last,
but when I sleep, I dream hayfields.

Porcelain Dolls

Porcelain dolls never dance when we're looking;
nor do they sing when we wake up to listen.
They sit and they stare when we enter, not daring
to chance, e'er a word or a glance, that might hasten
the fright or the sight of their porcelain faces,
caught in the glisten and gleam of their secretive
smiles. Oh, we sleep all the while they tie laces
to places that ought not be touched with such festive
and frolicking chases. These porcelain boys with

their porcelain girls, dancing on top of our cedar
chest bureaus. On some nights they dance and they swing with
their partners, their blue and white dresses flung higher
the faster they spin them. 'Tis true that they stand by
their story, that they never move from their places;
but surely they throw a gay ball when we sleep – I
can tell by the smile on their porcelain faces.

A good way to get a feel for how metre works is to practise *scanning*. Scanning occurs when we read poetry with exaggerated emphasis on the stressed syllables to determine its metre. If a poem does not have a regular metrical pattern it is said 'to not scan'. Try the following: Choose two or three examples of 'traditional' or metred poetry. Most nineteenth-century poetry will provide good material for this. Photocopy the poems and 'scan' them, marking the stressed and unstressed syllables. If scanning proves difficult at first, try it with a traditional nursery rhyme such as 'Jack and Jill', tapping your fingers to mark the stressed beats.

Why metre matters

Many contemporary poets take pride in rejecting metre – and there is certainly no shortage of amateurish attempts to imitate the metre of English poetry of previous centuries which continues to give metre a bad name. But English is a stressed language and our natural speech contains all sorts of metrical patterns. Good poets will be aware of these patterns and be able to use them well when needed, and avoid them when not. Neither is possible without a solid understanding of metre. In other words, if you want to write non-metred, or free-verse poetry well, then you still need to learn the basics of metre.

Exercise: Getting into the rhythm

The most common form of traditional English poetry is iambic pentameter. Construct a poem about some aspect of the natural world consisting of two quatrains (8 lines) in iambic pentameter with a regular rhyme scheme. The following is my attempt at this exercise. Once you gain a feel for the metre it is not difficult.

Drought-breaker

Angelic trump of fast abating thirst
As dark clouds roll across the western hills.
The droplets fall unpromising at first,
Then driving waves and mud-encrusted swills.

The moisture sweeps across the sun-parched earth,
Restoring life to couch and daffodils.
This precious water spreading now its girth,
Cut loose from banks, baptising while it kills.

Chapter 4:

Rhymes, Chimes and other Crimes

> *'The concept of rhyme was unknown to the Greeks, and rhyme was not used in classical poetry. Rhyme first came into use in the church Latin of North Africa around A.D. 200 in certain hymns and chants. By the fourth century, rhymed sacred poetry had spread ... and become a real stylistic movement in church liturgy.'*
>
> – Francis Stillman[1]

Rhyme

We tend to think of rhyme as a natural part of poetry, but many languages do not employ rhyme. The use of rhyme, in the sense that we have come to know it, actually comes from Christian hymn writers from North Africa in the second century. One might say, therefore, that modern rhyme is a Christian contribution to poetry – though given the current reputation of rhyme and its notorious misuse and abuse, not all Christian poets will be happy to take credit for this achievement.

There are many ways to rhyme a poem. Rhyme patterns might mean that each pair of lines (a couplet) rhyme with each other. We designate this as an aa-bb-cc pattern. Or perhaps every second line rhymes, in which case the rhyme pattern is ab-ab-cd-cd. Rhyme patterns can be complex and subtle, so that rhymes can be several lines apart from one another, and not every line needs to rhyme. These more subtle rhyming patterns have the effect of making the poem less 'sing-songy,' yet the subconscious still picks up on the repetition of the strong sound at the end of the lines.

Note the effect of metre and rhyme in the following list poem, in which only the final name carries any semantic meaning. This type of poem illustrates the beauty and impact the sounds of words can have apart

1 Francis Stillman. *The Poet's Manual and Rhyming Dictionary* (London: Thames and Hudson, 1966), 32.

from their meaning. And for the literary detective, there is an allusion in the poem to a famous Australian literary controversy. Can you spot it?[2]

Poets, Novelists, Playwrights, Bards

Auden, Longfellow, Bradford, Crane,
    Browning, Addison, Byron, Twain,
Chaucer, Tennyson, Cooper, Knight,
    Dickens, Malory, Channing, Wright,
Ellis, Parkinson, Shelley, Roe,
    Faulkner, Coleridge, Steinbeck, Poe,
Ginsberg, Stevenson, Baldwin, Smith,
    Hawthorne, Eliot, Boswell, Swift,
Irving, Hemingway, Winthrop, Scott,
    Jackson, Bradbury, Whitman, Locke,
Kipling, Chesterton, Manning, White,
    Lewis, Andersen, Mather, Bright,
Milton, Dickinson, Cummings, Bierce,
    Newman, Wigglesworth, Carlyle, Peirce,
Orwell, Thackeray, Bunyan, Gray,
    Parker, Kavanagh, Barlow, Ray,
Quincy, Christensen, Taylor, Pound,
    Rawling, Paterson, Tyson, Browne,
Sandburg, Harrington, Marlowe, Keats,
    Tolkien, Rowlandson, Melville, Yeats,
Updike, Tomlinson, Pratchett, Marsh,
    Vidal, Emerson, Pullman, Walsh,
Wordsworth, Ellison, Malley, Bryce,
    Xanthos, Berryman, Martel, Price,
Yoder, Ferguson, Heller, Young,
    Zafón, Sullivan, Huxley, Donne.

2 If you are having trouble working this one out, think Max Harris and *Angry Penguins*.

Exercise: List poem

Construct a poem using a list of names or items such as cities, foods, famous sports people, etc. in which the meaning of words plays no role, but only the metre, rhyme, alliterations, etc. of the sounds in the words or names. For an additional example of such a poem, see the 'Shaker Abecedarius' from the *Shaker Manifesto* of 1882 (cited in chapter 9).

Rhymes normally occur in fixed patterns at the end of lines. Some modern poetry will use occasional, unpatterned end rhymes, or rhymes that occur in the middle of lines. One popular form of Vietnamese poetry, for instance, has a rhyme not just at the end of each line, but two syllables from the end of every second line where the sound is not so striking, yet clearly noticeable.

There are also possibilities for double and triple rhymes. These occur when the poet rhymes not only the last syllables of key words but also the preceding syllable or syllables. For instance, 'syllable' and 'viable' constitute a double rhyme, and 'incantation' and 'implantation' form a triple rhyme. For most poems, however, more than the occasional use of a double or triple rhyme is far too heavy. Even single rhymes can become overwhelming and distracting when not used well. But this does not need to be the case.

In many instances, the excessive effect of regular rhyme can be mollified by use of either light rhyme or near rhyme. *Light rhyme* occurs when full rhyme is used, but the final syllable of one or more of the rhyming words is unstressed. This produces an effect that is more subtle than when the stress falls on final rhyming syllables. *Near rhymes* can also be light, but more generally are fully stressed approximate rhymes. For instance 'French' and 'hunch' do not form a perfect rhyme, but are close enough to produce a rhyming effect. Other near rhymes can be even further removed, for instance 'some' and 'song,' 'stifling' and 'being,' 'dread' and 'fixated.'

The following poem by W.H. Auden is a brilliant example of the effective use of what is often called half rhymes. In Auden's poem, the first and final consonants of the last syllable of each line rhyme in a simple aa-bb-cc pattern, but the final vowel sounds do not. Also, note the irregular iambic metre and the placement of major grammatical breaks in the middle of many lines (called enjambment). This has the effect of taking the focus off the end rhymes and further softening the rhyming effect.

Walking Tour

To throw away the key and walk away,
Not abrupt exile, the neighbours asking why,
But following a line with left and right
An altered gradient at another rate
Learns more than maps upon the whitewashed wall
The hand put up to ask; and makes us well
Without confession of the ill. All pasts
Are single old past now, although some posts
Are forwarded, held looking on a new view;
The future shall fulfil a surer vow
Not smiling at queen over the glass rim
Nor making gunpowder in the top room,
Not swooping at the surface still like gulls
But with prolonged drowning shall develop gills.

But there are still to tempt; areas not seen
Because of blizzards or an erring sign
Whose guessed-at wonders would be worth alleging,
And lies about the cost of a night's lodging.
Travellers may sleep at inns but not attach,
They sleep one night together, not asked to touch;
Receive no normal welcome, not the pressed lip,
Children to lift, not the assuaging lap.
Crossing the pass descend the growing stream
Too tired to hear except the pulses' strum,
Reach villages to ask for a bed in
Rock shutting out the sky, the old life done.[3]

3 W.H. Auden, 'Walking Tour,' in *Chief Modern Poets of Britain and America*, vol. 2. Ed. G. DeWitt Sanders, J.H. Nelson and M.L. Rosenthal. (London: Macmillan, 1972), 353.

Alliteration, assonance and consonance

Closely related to the use of rhyme in poetry are alliteration, assonance and consonance. *Alliteration* occurs when the first sounds of words in succession or close proximity begin with the same or similar sound. Tongue twisters are formed around the principle of alliteration, as in 'she sells seashells by the seashore.' *Assonance* occurs when the vowels in words rhyme but not the consonants. Assonance may also occur when a series of words repeats the same vowel sounds as for instance in, 'hear the mellow wedding bells,' from *The Bells* by Edgar Allen Poe. Similarly, *consonance* is the repetition of the consonantal sounds without the repetition of vowel sounds. An example is the repetition of 'd' sounds in the sentence; 'Daniel stood at the side of the road and cried'.

Tips for making rhyme work in contemporary poetry

There is no doubt that rhyme has fallen under a cloud in much of modern poetry. While it has always had its detractors (e.g., Milton), much of the best poetry in the English language, up until recent times, has been rhymed. Nowadays when someone speaks of rhymed poetry we tend to think of doggerel (rhymed, unmetred verse associated with amateurish efforts), greeting cards and overly pious religious verse. Rhyme has suffered from overuse, and the propensity to choose words that are all too common and obvious. But rhyme still has a place in contemporary poetry, and occurs sometimes even in what we might otherwise consider free verse. There is something very satisfying with finishing a key line or phrase with an effective rhyme. Conversely, poorly chosen rhyme can make your poem sound cheesy and amateurish. The following tips can be employed to use rhyme in a way that moderates this unfortunate effect.

1. Choose uncommon or unexpected words. Use a good rhyming dictionary for this. Everyone knows that red rhymes with bed, said and head, and blue is expected to be followed by true and you. Take the time to seek out the lesser-known or unexpected rhyming word.
2. Employ an irregular rhyme scheme. a-b-a-b, a-a-b-b, and a-b-b-a are common and regular rhyme patterns. Perhaps only two lines of your traditional quatrain (a four-line stanza) could rhyme, with the other two being blank verse (unrhymed). Or a pattern could be employed

that separates the rhymes by two or more lines. Or the rhymes could appear in a more occasional way throughout the poem so that the reader is not expecting one at the end of each line.

3. Use light rhyme. Most rhymes occur with a final stressed syllable. This accentuates the rhyme and its effect. If the final rhyming syllable is unstressed, say at the end of a true trochaic metred line, the rhyme sound is blunted.
4. Use near rhymes. While some see such rhymes as options when nothing better can be found, a near rhyme can give the satisfaction of a rhymed effect without sounding so obvious or sing-song. Words in which only the consonantal sounds rhyme (e.g., duck and like, hole and hill) or words in which only the vowel sounds rhyme (e.g., peek and seed) work well in many cases. There are words that also sound similar, though there is neither a pure consonantal nor assonantal rhyme. For instance, pyramids and legs work because both the vowel and consonant sounds are similar, and with the final 's', this effect is further heightened.
5. Enjambment. Enjambment occurs when the major grammatical break or pause occurs not at the end of a line but in the middle, hence preventing the reader from pausing at the rhyming word at the end of the line. There are several effective uses of enjambment in Auden's poem *Walking Tour* (cited above). Notice how they work to further 'hide' the rhymes at the end of the lines.

Chapter 5:

Shapes, Sounds and Syllables

> *'Poetry depends for its effectiveness on the union of sound and sense, word-shape and meaning, association and feeling. The cadence of the human voice, the "music" of sounds in sequence, the arresting freshness of images, the combination of emotion and idea – these give poetry its impact.'*
>
> – Colin Thiele[1]

Syllabics

Syllabics are a type of poem in which lines are measured not by metre but by the number of syllables per line. These can be regular or irregular patterns. The most famous of syllabic forms is the Haiku, which originated in Japan many centuries ago. Haiku has become popular as a teaching tool, and most school students have given it a try. One of the purposes of students learning Haiku is to teach concision of language and a sense of symmetry. While the style of the Haiku cannot be replicated exactly outside of Japanese, it follows a pattern of three lines of five, seven, and five syllables, respectively. The idea is that the last line should have some insight that interprets the whole poem. The classic example of Haiku is from the sixteenth-century poet Moritake. He wrote the following in reference to the Buddhist proverb that a fallen blossom never returns to the branch.

> The falling flower
> I saw drift back to the branch
> was a butterfly.

For those who find the Haiku too brief, a related Japanese form is the Tanka, which is essentially a Haiku, but with two additional lines of seven

---

1 Colin Thiele, 'Poetry and the Magic of Words,' in *Word Magic. Poetry as a Shared Adventure, ed. Walter McVitty* (Rozelle, NSW: PETA, 1985), 2

syllables each. Many poets writing in English have sought to achieve a similar effect of brevity with various other combinations.

Exercise: Succinctly syllabic

Choosing a simple theme, write a Haiku (or try several) that moves from everyday, common observation to a more pointed conclusion.

In modern English poetry, syllabic poems are often quite complex, as with the verse of American poet Marianne Moore. Often a stanza of several lines of varying lengths appears quite random, but the syllabic pattern is then repeated in each successive stanza. In the following segment from Moore's poem *The Plumet Basilisk* (1935), notice the syllabic pattern in each stanza of 5-9-14-12-16, the rhyming of lines two and four, and the tendency to continue a sentence or phrase onto the following line (enjambment).

The Tuatera

Elsewhere, sea lizards –
  congregated so there is not room
to step, with tails laid criss-cross, alligator-style, among
  birds toddling in and out – are innocent of whom
they neighbour. Bird-reptile social life is pleasing. The tuatera

will tolerate a
  petrel in its den, and lays ten eggs
or nine – the number laid by dragons since 'a true dragon
  has nine sons.' The frilled lizard, the kind with no legs,
and the three-horned chameleon, are non-serious ones that take to flight

if you do not. In
  Copenhagen the principal door
of the bourse is roofed by two pairs of dragons standing on
  their heads – twirled by the architect – so that the four
green tails conspiring upright, symbolize four-fold security.[2]

2 Marianne Moore. *The Complete Poems* (Penguin Books, 1986), 21.

Shape poems

Written poetry is also able to take advantage of a number of visual effects. Poetry that relies on the shape or layout of the words on the page to help convey the meaning or impact of the poem is called shape (or concrete) poetry. Poems can be written in such a way as to form a shape appropriate to the theme, as in the following triangular ode to the Trinity – which is also a triplet of rhymed, syllabic poems.

De Trinitate

God
Father
Who is he
Judge we all bless
Who views creation
Each sinful soul no less
In such compassion
That we confess
She must be
Mother
God.

Son
From high
One with God
From heaven's rule
Who was born to bear
Our sins on Roman cross
Upon which he did hear
A p e a s a n t girl
C r y a l o u d
'That's my
Son!'

Breath
Set free
I wonder
Why we do fear
You who comes as dove
To comfort those who hear
The message of love
That God is near
Within our
E v e r y
Breath.

Also, the way the lines are formed on the page can express or reinforce the ideas in the poem, as in the following example:

Time

Appointments,
duties,
deadlines
pile
up

like seething water
waiting to tumble
over
the
precipice,
falling
ever
down-
ward
into the mists of
the unknown –
fragments of our lives
s w e p t   a w a y
in the flow of time.

Exercise: Writing to form

Try a simple shape poem. Choose a theme or item that has a recognisable shape, for instance a vase. Draw the shape roughly in your notebook. Write a description of a vase (perhaps some particular vase, e.g., Grecian, Chinese, one with flowers in it, etc.) so that the lines fit within the outline of the vase you've drawn. As you transfer the poem to your computer, centre each line and see how close you've come to the vase shape you sought to achieve. You may have to alter some lines or add additional spaces between some words to highlight the effect.

Onomatopoetic effects

Many words in our language are formed to reflect or mimic the sound of the thing they describe. Other words, by accident or design, sound like that which they represent. When this occurs the effect is called *onomatopoeia.* Using such words or combinations of words creates strong effects in poetry. Gentle words are the best choices when describing something soft, lovely or soothing. Harsh words work best when describing something more violent, brash or rugged.

One of the most famous uses of onomatopoeia in poetry is by Edgar Allan Poe in *The Raven.* The rapping and tapping, repeated in the poem, sounds like the raven's beak on the window pane. It is one of the reasons the poem is so memorable. The first stanza grabs our attention and makes us feel we are there, hearing the tapping.

> Once upon a midnight dreary, while I pondered, weak and weary,
> Over many a quaint and curious volume of forgotten lore—
>   While I nodded, nearly napping, suddenly there came a tapping,
> As of someone gently rapping, rapping at my chamber door.
> "'Tis some visitor," I muttered, "tapping at my chamber door—
>   Only this and nothing more."

Listen carefully to the sound and pattern of words in the following poem that describes a windstorm from the perspective of someone taking shelter in a farmhouse. Try to identify the words that are onomatopoetic.

The Blow

First a gentle humming,
then a rustling
and a rushing;
leaf and limb dancing
faster and faster.
The fiddler laughs;
they cannot keep

his rhythm,
his pace.
They snap
and join fallen partners,
not dancing
but driven.
Horses stampeding.
Bleeding faces
of house, barn and hill.
Sand and leaves
caught up in growing
unbearable drone.
Waves walk
through air;
knocking,
hammering,
battering,
Window and door.
A giant hand
sweeps across the earth.
Sugar Gum and shed
crash to the ground.
Some young deity
in violent tantrum
clears a playing board
of useless pieces.
Sand, leaves, limbs, fear
regroup
in one last assault,
a final charge.
A train thunders
toward the house.
Windows and walls bow,
curtains cling,
uncertain ceiling.
Everything trembles . . .

hesitates.
BANG!
goes the front
picture window.
Hearts stop,
fingers clench,
children scream.
Glass slaps
against walls,
then slides
to the floor.
Fireworks
drift to earth
in slow motion.
Walls straighten,
curtains fall –
then stillness
and quiet.
It is over.

CHAPTER 6:

Poetry Unshackled – Free Verse

'The first rule of poetry is that there are no rules.'

– Anonymous

'Free verse is not totally free. Its only freedom is from the tyrant demands of the metred line.'

– Allen Charles[1]

Free verse is deceptively simple to produce. There are no fixed rules of metre and rhyme to follow. Some disparage this form as the death knell of poetry. Others welcome it as a breath of fresh air, making poetry writing accessible to a greater number of people and freeing it from the constraints of rigid forms. There is a bit of truth in both views. While the aversion to traditional forms has led to a loss of variety and technical competence in some modern poetry, traditional forms had become rather stale and predictable by the late nineteenth century, and some form of revolt was inevitable.

French poets Arthur Rimbaud (1854-1891) and Jules Laforgue (1860-1887) are commonly credited with pioneering *vers libre* (free verse). But their American predecessor Walt Whitman (1819-1892) probably deserves equal credit for his non-rhyming, non-metred style of verse made famous in successive editions of *Leaves of Grass*.[2] Not only did Whitman's poetry represent a radical shift in style, it also signalled a shift in theme. Whitman's verse celebrated nature, the human self and human sexuality in ways that changed modern poetry. The opening poem in Whitman's collection, 'One's-self I sing,' stands as a manifesto of the modern individual.

One's-self I sing, a simple separate person,
Yet utter the word Democratic, the word En-Masse.

1 Allen Charles, 'Cadenced Free Verse,' in *College English* vol 9, no. 6 (January 1948).

2 And Whitman and others were, in turn, likely influenced by the 'free verse' of the Bible. See John Whitworth, *Writing Poetry*, 2nd ed. (London: A and C Black, 2006), 95.

Of physiology from top to toe I sing,
Not physiognomy alone nor brain alone is worthy for the Muse,
    I say the Form complete is worthier far,
The female equally with the Male I sing.

Of life immense in passion, pulse, and power,
Cheerful, for freest action form'd under the laws divine,
The Modern Man I sing.[3]

One criticism of free verse is that it is only distinguishable from prose because it is set out in verse form. This, of course, is far from the case. Yet free verse does pose the question, 'What is the precise boundary between poetry and prose?' It is well known that many delightful 'found' poems can be discovered hidden in the midst of quality works of prose fiction. Here is an example taken from *The Book Thief* by Markus Zusak.[4]

> A human doesn't have a heart like mine. The human heart is a line whereas my own is a circle, and I have the endless ability to be in the right place at the right time. The consequences of this is that I'm always finding humans at their best and worst. I see their ugly and their beauty, and I wonder how the same thing can be both. Still, they have one thing that I envy. Humans if nothing else, have the good sense to die.

It can be set out in verse, without altering the wording or punctuation, as follows, highlighting the inherent poetry of this passage.

Death's Monologue

A human
doesn't have a heart
like mine.

3 Walt Whitman. *Leaves of Grass* (New York: Airmont Publishing, 1965), 21.
4 Markus Zusak, *The Book Thief* (Sydney: Macmillan, 2005).

The human heart
is a line
whereas my own
is a circle, and
I have the endless
ability to be
in the right place
at the right time.
The consequences of this is that
I'm always finding
humans
at their best and worst.
I see their ugly
and their beauty,
and I wonder how the same thing
can be both.
Still,
they have one thing that I envy.
Humans
if nothing else,
have the good sense
to die.

The fact that poetry can be 'discovered' in works of prose fiction does not mean there is little or no distinction between free verse and prose. It demonstrates only that very good writers often express their thoughts poetically, even in prose form. Certainly there is an art to how lines are divided for effect, but good 'found' poetry cannot be taken simply from any portion of any prose work. While Zusak is a very good writer with vivid imagery, I had to look through the novel carefully to find these poignant sentences. The repetition of key words, like 'human,' or similar phrases, like 'right place/right time,' the alliteration 'human' and 'heart' in the first four lines, and natural rhymes like 'ugly' and 'beauty,' all help to make this particular piece a good found poem, as well as a beautiful piece of prose.

Exercise: Create a 'found' poem

Select a novel or other piece of enjoyable prose you have recently read. Look for some memorable section of description, action, etc. and lay out the sentences in verse form. You will find that not every section of prose is well-suited for this. The exercise is also good for gaining a feel for the importance of line division in free verse.

Free verse, like any form of poetry, can find its inspiration anywhere. A few years ago I was in a large city bookstore and had a rather unusual experience. I had my notebook with me so jotted down the details while they were fresh. When I arrived home and had a chance to look over my notes I found that I liked their unstructured feel, so decided to make only minor modifications. The end result was the following free-verse poem.

Bookstore Schizophrenic

'Not 'til she's dead, I swear,
not 'til she's dead,'
rang the agitated voice
from the reference section
across travel, self-help and fiction.
'Tell her whatever you want,
I'm not coming back 'til she's dead.'

The old man perusing home and garden
shook his head
'Inconsiderate youth of today,'
he said to no one in particular,
re-shelving his book
as he shuffled off
toward the religion section.

‘Look, Bro, she’s my mother too’
– the voice now more intense –
‘But after what she’s done to us,
you know, to me and to you,
I’ll not come back ’til she’s dead.’

I tried to concentrate meanwhile
on the volume on Freud I’d found
two rows over,
as intriguing as one half
of mobile reality can be.

The young man’s voice was lower now,
its intermittent, short replies more subdued.
‘They should check those things at the door,’
said the old man, ambling past again,
having apparently found nothing of interest in religion.
But his peace and mine
was short-lived as a summer rain.
‘Bloody Rann. Made my life hell, he has.
I’ll never vote Labor again!’

Good Lord, I thought, now he’s onto politics.
For a quarter of an hour – though it seemed more –
I endured half a conversation
on economics, sanctions and the Iraq war,
‘Til I decided – against my nature –
that some action must be taken.
I’d duck into his aisle and give him a
cool stare (that’s what I’d do).
But I must admit I was unprepared
for the scruffed young man
reading the *Oxford English Dictionary* –
no mobile in hand –
though still in a huff over Premier Rann,
talking, like the old man in home and garden,
to no one in particular –
just another bookstore schizophrenic.

The reality is that free verse is not always as free as it seems. In the best examples there is much going on, subtly. In fact, the best free verse is often produced by those who are gifted structuralists. Pablo Picasso was once asked how he was able to paint a horse that didn't look like a horse. He responded that one first had to learn how to paint a horse that looked like a horse. There is a difference between modern paintings that are deliberately abstract, and those that are abstract because the painter lacks the skills to do otherwise. The distinction may be subtle, but it is often the difference between great modern art and parody. The situation with poetry is similar. If you wish to write great free verse, first learn how to write more structured forms of poetry well. You should write free verse because you choose to, not because it's the only form you are able to write.

I remember having an animated conversation with a promising young poet a few years back who had already had several poems published in recognised poetry journals and collections. He claimed he wrote only in free verse because other forms were tired, too constricted and simply didn't have anything to offer. I asked him if he knew how to construct, or at least recognise a sonnet. He did not. I asked him if he knew what a sestina was. He did not. I asked him if he had ever tried to write a syllabic (other than a Haiku). He had not. I asked him if he knew how to scan a poem for metre. He did not. Finally, I told him that perhaps writing exclusively in free verse was a considered choice on his part, but so long as he remained ignorant of all other forms, I was inclined to believe that he had little other choice but to write only in free verse. Oh, and the animated discussion we were having? It began when I asked him whether the two lines of iambic metred verse in the poem he had asked me to look at were intended. They were not.

The following is an example of a free verse poem in which there is much happening structurally. It is the first stanza of a much longer poem, celebrating the letters of the alphabet. Each stanza consists of twenty-six lines, and a key word or words in the final line of each stanza is picked up in the first line of the next stanza. How many structural and literary devices you can find in this stanza of 'free' verse. As T. S. Eliot said, no verse is entirely free.[5]

---

5 T.S. Eliot, 'Reflections on *Vers Libre*' (1917), in *The Structure of Verse*, ed. Harvey Gross (The Ecco Press, 1979).

A

A, Aleph, Alpha
grown into runic Anglo oak;
ancient astrological ox,
horns turned down for headlong charge
through newly formed alphabet.
Or is it Victor Hugo's two friends shaking hands
in mid embrace – an alphabetic canopy?
Algebraic known quantity 'a'
or all-creating Alpha and Omega,
symbol of God's tripartite unity.
From beginning to end, we race,
laughing through Seuss's abecedary and
Aunt Annie's alligators asking Alice
whether Hester Prynne can ever forgive
the dark side of A,
begun for all in Adam's fall.
Meanwhile Andrew Aguecheek,
with no more wit than a Christian speaks;
'Abracadabra, Open Sesame.'
Big A, little a,
anaphoric key to childhood literacy –
literary celebrity:
Monarch Aleph, Jacob Grimm's king of vowels
and Hegel's pyramids,
or simply Wallace Steven's
infant A, standing on infant legs.[6]

When writing free verse, line division is vital. Try dividing your lines in different places to see the effect. Often the division will fall along natural grammatical lines, such as the end of a phrase or sentence. But try to avoid doing this with each line. Also, you will not be relying on rhyme patterns and metre for the poetic feel of your verse, so you will need to give special attention to such things as alliteration, assonance and

6 Mark Worthing. *Abecedarium. A Celebration of the Alphabet in Verse* (Adelaide: Immortalise, 2019), 4.

consonance. But be careful not to overdo these. It is like adding seasoning to a stew. Too much of a good thing will spoil the broth. Play with sounds, work with visual images, metaphors, and allusions. Experiment. Find a style, rhythm and voice that work for you and your themes.

Exercise: Vers Libre

Choose a theme expressing some particular emotion (love, anger, frustration, etc.) and write a poem in free verse. The lines should not be prose, but should consist of 'chunks' of thought that when read aloud fall naturally into individual units of poetic line. Alliteration, word play, sounds that have a desired impact, metaphor and vivid imagery are all encouraged in moderation. But there should be no regular metre, syllabic structure or rhyme.

CHAPTER 7:

Rediscovering Structure in Poetry

> *'Poems are part of the memory of the human race. But, to become part of memory, a poem has to be memorable. How? For Ted Hughes it was the sound that did it – the rhymes and rhythms ... with an insistent beat.'*
>
> – John Whitworth[1]

The New Structuralism

Structural forms, long out of fashion, have been making a comeback in recent decades. Fortunately, this has not simply meant a return to the sonnet and iambic pentameter with regular rhyme schemes. The new structuralist stream has tended to be more nuanced, less bound to rigid rules, often masking metre and rhyme, or breaking them up unexpectedly. The poem at the end of this section, *The Poetic Circle*, is an example. It may at first appear to contain little structure, but a closer look reveals much use of alliteration and consonance, a thematic structure that comes full-circle to themes from the beginning of the poem, a tight syllabic structure, and a regular rhyme scheme.

Some have sought to rediscover and explore more exotic structural forms. The following poem, which appeared in *The New Formalism in Poetry*[2] is highly structured. The form is a *pantoum*, which is Malayan in origin. It calls for the second and fourth lines of each quatrain (four-line stanza) to be repeated as the first and third lines of the following stanza. Finally, the first and third lines of the first quatrain are repeated as the second and fourth lines of the last quatrain. What appealed to me about the form was the clever use of repetition. Repetition always brings with it a certain poetic feel, but to use each line twice, and each time in a different, and often opposite sense, while progressing the movement of

1 John Whitworth, *Writing Poetry*, 1.

2 M. Worthing, 'Pantoum for Little Crow,' in *The MacGuffin: The New Formalism in Poetry* 7:2 1990, 123ff.

the entire poem, is a considerable challenge. While difficult to construct, the form lends itself well to humour and satire, or in the following case, biting critique.

Pantoum for Little Crow[3]

Tshe-ton Wa-ka-wa Ma-ni,
    Shot picking red raspberries;
The Hawk That Hunts Walking,
    In the Moon of Red Blooming Lilies.

Shot picking red raspberries;
Twenty-five dollars for Sioux scalps;
In the Moon of Red Blooming Lilies,
    Like Buffalo, Fox or Beaver pelts.

Twenty-five dollars for Sioux scalps;
    In July when Little Crow died,
Like Buffalo, Fox or Beaver pelts,
    The summer the Santee Sioux cried.

In July when Little Crow died,
    Twenty-five dollars bought meat;
The summer the Santee Sioux cried,
    Flour and pork were cheap.

Twenty-five dollars bought meat,
    At the Medicine River Agency,
Flour and pork were cheap,
    For agents with Indian money.

At the Medicine River Agency,
    The flour and grain price was low,
For agents with Indian money,
    The summer before they shot Little Crow.

---

3 The tragic story of the death of Little Crow can be found in Dee Brown, *Bury My Heart at Wounded Knee*: *An Indian History of the American West*. (New York: Bantam, 1972).

The flour and grain price was low,
    When Myrick said Sioux should eat grass;
The summer before they shot Little Crow,
    When starvation was coming on fast.

When Myrick said Sioux should eat grass,
    Little Crow launched his hungry war;
When starvation was coming on fast,
    The Mdewkantons trusted no more.

Little Crow launched his hungry war,
    Driven by legal government theft;
The Mdewkantons trusted no more,
    Forced to choose between exile and death.

Driven by legal government theft,
    The Bluecoats rode in like lightning;
Forced to choose between exile and death,
    The Santee chose to die fighting.

The Bluecoats rode in like lightning,
    In the Wild Rice Moon of sixty-two;
The Santee chose to die fighting,
    Little Crow led the Santee Sioux.

In the Wild Rice Moon of sixty-two,
When many brave warriors had died,
Little Crow led the Santee Sioux,
    When no place was left safe to hide.

When many brave warriors had died,
Some chose surrender instead;
When no place was left safe to hide,
    Little Crow took his family and fled.

Some chose surrender instead;
Their gallows were built in December.
Little Crow took his family and fled,
    The great chief we choose not remember.

Their gallows were built in December,
And Little Crow shot for a bounty,
The great chief we choose not remember;
    Much less than they promised in treaty.

And Little Crow shot for a bounty,
For twenty-five dollars that bought,
Much less than they promised in treaty,
    Much more than Little Crow sought.

For twenty-five dollars that bought,
A Christian and civilised wake;
Much more than Little Crow sought,
    Impaled on a hickory stake.

A Christian and civilised wake,
In St. Paul where dead he lay;
Impaled on a hickory stake,
    His scalp and his skull on display.

In St. Paul where dead he lay,
They didn't know what to call,
His scalp and his skull on display,
    Soaring in death above all.

They didn't know what to call,
Tshe-ton Wa-ka-wa Ma-ni;
Soaring in death above all,
    The Hawk That Hunts Walking.

Other forms that you may wish to try your hand at include:

Ballad. The ballad is a longer poem consisting of an undefined number of quatrains; that is, it can be as long as you wish it to be. The ballad normally tells a story, so attention must be given to the narrative flow. The first and third lines are four feet and unrhymed. The second and fourth lines are three feet each and rhymed.

Sonnet. There are various forms of the sonnet, usually set apart by differing rhyme schemes. All sonnets have fourteen lines, often set out as three quatrains and a final couplet. Most sonnets are in iambic pentameter. Perhaps best known is the Shakespearean sonnet, with a rhyme scheme of a-b-a-b, c-d-c-d, e-f-e-f, g-g.

Rondel. This popular medieval form originated in France. Like the sonnet, it is fourteen lines in length. It consists of two quatrains, followed by two tercets (three line stanzas). The rondel is similar to the pantoum in that the form makes use of repetition of lines. In the rondel the first and second lines are repeated as lines seven and eight, and finally as lines thirteen and fourteen. The metre pattern may vary.

Villanelle. Another medieval French invention, the villanelle resembles in many ways the rondel. It consists of five tercets and a final quatrain. The first and third lines of the first tercet alternate as the final lines of the following tercets, so that the second tercet ends with repeating line one, and the third tercet ends with repeating line three, the fourth with line one again, the fifth with line three, and the final quatrain ends with lines one and three as the final lines of the poem. Hence the lines repeat as follows: 1-2-3; x-x-1; x-x-3; x-x-1; x-x-3; x-x-1-3.

Sestina. Once more, another medieval French innovation. The sestina is a blank verse (unrhymed) poem of six stanzas with six lines in each stanza. The trick is that the same final six words of the lines are used in each stanza, but in a varying order. The order in which the final words are repeated is as follows: 1-2-3-4-5-6; 6-1-5-2-4-3; 3-6-4-1-2-5; 5-3-2-6-1-4; 4-5-1-3-6-2; 2-4-6-5-3-1. Notice the last word of line six in each stanza becomes the last word in the first line of the following stanza, and that the last word of the first and final lines of the poem are the same. Traditionally, this form is metered.

The following sestina explores the story of the Good Samaritan. It makes use of anagrams for the final set of six words. The use of anagrams is not necessary for the sestina, but was done here to give the poem a semi-rhyming feel as the six end words are not only repeated, but also employ similar sounds and provide something of a *sight rhyme* effect as well.

Samaritan Sestina

A wand'ring figure walking fast beside a weary donkey tops
a hard-climbed crest, with wares of earthen pots.
He leads his beast on treacherous trail to stop,
reluctant and afraid, at recently disturbed and dusty spot
where half-dead lay a bloodied man against a post.
Despite his culture, faith and better sense he opts –

In truth, against ingrained long years of fear and hate he opts –
to aid a stiff-necked, battered Jew who tops
his tight held list of enemies. It takes a further glance or two to spot
the signs of roguish ambush that had brought to sudden stop
the victim's outbound journey. So the merchant brings his rattling pots
to halt; by blighted, blood-stained palm stump post.

This merchant of Samaria takes up a tenûous post
beside the slumped and swollen stranger whom he opts
to aid. His stoppered leather water flask he tops,
and pours its cool and cleansing contents over every spot
of flayéd flesh to bring the blood flow to a stop.
The merchant, shrugging, with a frown, turns once more to his pots.

From humble beast he lets fall free his load of valued pots,
so making room for one still slumped against the post.
Despite the waste of hard-won wares he opts
to help a Jew whom he knew not. He tops
his unsought show of mercy on that wastrel spot
by bringing now his own intended journey to a stop.
The long-fought feud 'twixt Jew and heretic must momentarily stop,

for no fine load of Jericho-turned earthen pots –
nor long embittered history that all diminished expectation tops –
will halt this unrequited act of kindness that our lonely trader opts
to give, when his own burdened beast and soul he brings to post,
revealing pity seldom seen in this or other spot.

His face now fixed upon his course, he leaves that fated spot
and travels 'til he brings his lumbering beast to stop
at isolated inn, wherein he might have hoped to sell his pots.
Outside the mudbrick stable, he ties his donkey fast to cedar post
and rouses then the publican, who with some urging at last opts
to keep his wounded countryman for two weeks, tops.

Hence mercy tops the worth of earthen pots
and brings a short-term stop to feuding on that spot
as wounded Jew is given post by heretic – who for mercy opts.

Limerick. Named after the town in Ireland, though it was likely invented elsewhere, the limerick is used almost entirely for humorous themes. It is a five-line verse with an a-a-b-b-a rhyme scheme. The metre is tricky, with the first, second and fifth lines containing three feet each consisting of one iamb followed by two anapests, and the third and fourth lines being anapestic dimeter. While complex, the form is familiar enough to most of us that it is quite easy to compose.

The following is an oft-cited, anonymous example of a double limerick, playing on the question of the relationship between God and the physical world.[4]

There was a young man who said God
Must think it exceedingly odd
If he finds that this tree
Continues to be
When there's no one about in the Quad.
Dear Sir, your astonishment's odd:

4 The poem is a tongue-in-cheek response to a statement made by George Berkeley in his 1710 treatise, *Concerning the Principles of Human Knowledge*, in which he claimed that a tree in a garden does not exist if there is no one present to perceive it.

I am always about in the Quad.
And that's why the tree
Will continue to be,
Since observed by yours faithfully, God

Exercise: Writing structured poetry

Try your hand at one of the traditional poetry forms described in this chapter. Pick a theme or a story and a structure to go with, then see if you are able to put the two together. You will be able find examples of the form you choose online. The task may seem at first overwhelming, but many find following a set form in some respects easier than starting with a blank pages, as much of the structure is already provided.

CHAPTER 8:

Writing Faith-themed Poetry

> *'One of the unaccountable assumptions about writing is that, though a person may lack both the ability to interpret life meaningfully and a knowledge of poetic forms, they can (they believe) sit down and write poetry which some editor will be delighted to publish. ... The sad thing is that God is often given credit for inspiring these 'masterpieces.'*
>
> – Margaret Anderson[1]

Have you ever cringed when someone's brought you a poem they've written about their faith? It is not that we are uninterested in either faith or poetry. Rather, it is the unfortunate reality that large amounts of poor poetry, often expressing a vague or misconstrued theology, are regularly produced under the guise of religious verse. We can easily forget that faith-based poetry can be very good poetry. The post-conversion religious verse of T. S. Eliot is a case in point. If your tastes lay more in the direction of classical forms, any decent hymnal will contain hundreds of metred and rhymed poems that are usually both well-crafted and theologically well thought out. But be careful not to simply try to replicate great religious hymnody of past centuries, as modern attempts to imitate these forms often fall short of the intended mark.

So how do we break free of the trap of writing well-meaning but nonetheless predictable expressions of our faith? Many avoid religious themes entirely in their poetry because of this association. But just because a theme may appear overdone, or too often done poorly, does not mean that it should be abandoned – especially a theme as rich and significant as our experience of God's grace. Certainly the Christian poet should be able to write about their faith experiences.

One helpful approach is to read good faith-themed poetry from a range of authors with various styles. This is a good way to discover the diversity of possibilities that exist for expressing our faith experiences in verse.

---

1 Margaret Anderson, *The Christian Writers' Handbook* (San Francisco: Harper & Row, 1974), 68.

Also, too often we seek to express a simple and easy-to-understand faith. In doing this we sometimes strip our poems of any ambiguity, nuance, struggle or artistry. This is a great pity. There are some gifted Christian poets writing today, and there is a need to express the wide range of faith experiences in poetic form. If you are inclined to express your experience of faith in verse, don't follow the easy and expected path. Consider the following points when you write:

1. Don't try to make your poem sound like a hymn – unless you are writing a hymn.
2. Don't be too obvious in the points you are making.
3. Avoid well-worn theological and religious words and expressions.
4. Deal with themes on the periphery of your faith experience. Not all poetry has to be specifically about Christ or prayer. Write about church architecture, Christian symbols, religious figures, the significance of the cross in the face of personal tragedy, your experience of doubt, etc.
5. Don't be overly (or even overtly) pious. It's okay to pose some tough questions, to show that you struggle, or even be a bit cheeky.

Judith Wright, a prominent twentieth-century Australian poet, produced one of the most thought-provoking reflections on the cross of Christ I have encountered. Importantly, the imagery is not always immediately clear, and the language is not the traditional language of Christian piety – or at least not used in the traditional way. Its title, the start of a quote from Jesus as he hung on the cross, is an indication of the theme of the poem.

Eli, Eli

To see them go by drowning in the river –
soldiers and elders drowning in the river,
the pitiful women drowning in the river,
the children's faces staring from the river –
that was his cross, and not the cross they gave him.

To hold the invisible wand, and not to save them –
to know them turned to death, and yet not save them;
only to cry to them and not to save them,
knowing that no one but themselves could save them –
this was the wound, more than the wound they dealt him.

To hold out love and know they would not take it,
to hold out faith and know they dared not take it –
the invisible wand, and none would see or take it,
all he could give, and there was none to take it –
thus they betrayed him, not with the tongue's betrayal.

He watched, and they were drowning in the river;
faces like sodden flowers in the river –
faces of children moving in the river;
and all the while, he knew there was no river.[2]

When we think of Christian poets, we cannot go past T.S. Eliot, whose poetry began to increasingly reflect religious themes after his mid-career conversion to Christianity. The meaning of his poems, cradled in striking imagery, is seldom immediately and indisputably clear. Eliot had an ability to express deep faith and also to raise troublesome questions in the same poem. The Ariel poems are good examples of this, of which *Song for Simeon* is one of my favourites. In this poem Eliot revisits a well-known biblical scene that has become embedded in our liturgy.

Lord, the Roman hyacinths are blooming in bowls and
The winter sun creeps by the snow hills;
The stubborn season had made stand.
My life is light, waiting for the death wind,
Like a feather on the back of my hand.
Dust in sunlight and memory in corners
Wait for the wind that chills towards the dead land.

---

2 Judith Wright. *Collected Poems* (Angus & Robertson, 1994), 44f.

Grant us thy peace.
I have walked many years in this city,
Kept faith and fast, provided for the poor,
Have given and taken honour and ease.
There went never any rejected from my door.
Who shall remember my house, where shall live my children's
  children
When the time of sorrow is come?
They will take to the goat's path, and the fox's home,
Fleeing from the foreign faces and the foreign swords.

Before the time of cords and scourges and lamentation
Grant us peace.
Before the stations of the mountain of desolation,
Before the certain hour of maternal sorrow,
Now at this birth season of decease,
Let the Infant, the still unspeaking and unspoken Word,
Grant Israel's consolation
To one who has eighty years and no tomorrow.

According to thy word.
They shall praise Thee and suffer in every generation
With glory and derision,
Light upon light, mounting the saints' stair.
Not for me the martyrdom, the ecstasy of thought and prayer,
Not for me the ultimate vision.
Grant me thy peace.
(And a sword shall pierce thy heart,
Thine also)
I am tired with my own life and the lives of those after me,
I am dying in my own death and the deaths of those after me.
Let thy servant depart in peace,
Having seen thy salvation.[3]

---

3 T.S. Eliot. *Collected Poems*. 1909-1962 (London: Faber and Faber, 1980), 111f.

I admit that I struggle to write about my faith in poetic form without it sounding trite or contrived. It is not easy. What follows is a poem that I felt achieved, in some small way, what I was trying to express. I wrote it in response to a journal entry I read from Hopkins, which in turn brought to remembrance a theological reflection from Teilhard de Chardin.[4]

Sunday, but no Catholics

Reluctant swung the oak-hewn door
in chaste response
to the young priest's touch.
Within lay narrow silent chapel
stripped of all but cruciform altar.
It was Sunday, but no Catholics
filled the mission parish;
Sunday, but no Catholics
to hear his mass;
Sunday, but no Catholics
to receive the Sacrament
from the hands of one
so willing. He filled
his chalice with wine
as wet as the blood
of a thousand martyrs – or One,
lifted up
from that crude chancel altar
for the whole thirsty world
to get drunk upon.
'The blood of Christ
shed for all,' he said,
and gulped it down. It was
Sunday, but no Catholics.

4 Inspired by the journal entry of Gerard Manly Hopkins of 19 July 1868, and Teilhard de Chardin, *Hymn of the Universe* (New York: Harper & Row, 1965) esp. 19ff. 'Since one again, Lord – though this time not in the forests of the Aisne but in the steppes of Asia – I have neither bread, nor wine, nor altar, I will raise myself beyond these symbols. .... I, your priest, will make the whole earth my altar and on it I will lay all the labours and sufferings of the world.'

Here is one from a former student, Caz Williams.[5]

You I

life is messy and complicated and hard
You provide for every need

I cry out my distress
You reply wordlessly

my skin hungers for a loving embrace
You enfold my soul with love

I stumble blindly
You guide my every step

I fall and cannot rise
You lie beside me

I cannot anticipate
You I
trust You

Exercise: Faith poems

Write a poem that touches upon some aspect of your faith. Take a different approach or use a different style. Find some event, object or experience that provides a way into the topic. Seek to express some aspect of your faith in such a way that your poem does not sound too predictable or familiar. Sometimes an atypical approach is more effective than a poem that sounds too much like a hymn or something from a greeting card.

---

5 From her unpublished collection, *Up is Down, Down is Lilac*.

CHAPTER 9:

Poetic Word Games

'Word games are the poet's gymnastics '

– John Whitworth[1]

While seldom rising to the level of emotive poetry, the combination of poetic forms with various word games can be a great fun. More importantly, they stretch our ability to work with and be attentive to words. In fact, it could be argued that poetry is little more than word games. Following are some examples of poetic word games. Give them a try, or invent your own. Such exercises are a great way of gaining mastery of different aspects of the language.

Homophones[2]

The English language contains a considerable number of words that sound like other words but are spelled differently and have different meanings (e.g., course and coarse, flea and flee) The following poem, in trochaic pentameter, makes sense (mostly) when heard, but not a single word looks right. The poem also reminds us of the importance of not relying on the spellcheck program on our computer!

Plane Two Here Butt Knot Sew Plane Too Sea

Deer Ant Sioux Kneel-sun
Inn Fare Whether Burro,

Eye due knot no weather eye herd yew write,
Ore dew eye no weather ewe bare yore pour cite.

1 John Whitworth, *Writing Poetry*, 27.

2 Note: *Homonyms* (though definitions vary) are words that are spelled the same and sound the same but have different meanings. These are often confused with *homophones*, which are words that sound the same, but are spelled differently and have different meanings. *Homographs* are word that are spelled the same but have different meanings and/or pronunciations.

Eye herd buy male wear yew eight yore pore hoarse,
Oar eight yore hoarse tale, inn won ore to coarse.
Butt weather ewe eight your pour hoarse oar hoarse tale,
Eye right two no weather yew sea yore male;
Four eye aught too no weather won tale ore to,
Wood bee aloud two dam hymn oar dam ewe.
Sew weather yew eight yore pore hoarse oar hoarse tale,
Ewe aught knot altar yore coarse oar yore male,
Weather ore knot yew Stu yore hoarse two knight.
Butt eye due knot no weather eye herd ewe write.

Sea yew inn to daze,
Yore Sun inn Plane Would.

Word scrambles

A report was circulated via email in 2003 claiming that a Cambridge University study suggested proper spelling is not particularly important for word recognition.[3] As long as the first and last letters are correct, and the other letters are all present, most readers can quickly recognise the intended word. The following lament for years spent learning proper spelling puts the theory to the test.

Srcamebld Wrods

Waht a wsate tohoght I, wehn I hread,
All thsoe yaers sepnt lnearnig persiceley
Teh porepr palce for erevy lteter in erevy wrod –
No eorrrs aollwed wehn oen witres cnosicely.

But wiat, say teh epxerts tihs weke psat,
It mtatres not hwo you sepll a wrod,

3 As it turned out, no such study had been conducted at Cambridge, but the report did spur several studies that suggested there might be something to this claim, though the reasons are unclear. Cf. Rebecca Johnson and Morgan Eisler, 'The Importance of the first and last letter in words during sentence reading, in *Acta Psychologica* (v. 141, 2012): 336-351; and K. Rayner, S. White, R. Johnson and S. Liversedge, 'Raeding wrods with jubmled lettres: There is a cost,' in *Psychological Science* (v. 17, 2006): 192-193.

So lnog as teh fisrt and lsat
lteters ecah are in teihr porper palce.

Ohter lteters can mnigle adn dncae aobut
a wrod hwoerver tehy palese,
Our eeys it semes dno't ralley crae
so lnog as ecah adn ervry lteter is tehre.

Clichés

Clichés as a rule should be avoided in good writing. But sometimes a cliché can be turned around (or inside out, if you prefer) with interesting effect. When I was a boy, reversible jackets were popular. When you got tired of one colour or pattern you simply turned the jacket inside out and had a whole new jacket. So why not, I thought, try the same thing with tired old clichés?

Cliché Reversibles

They say what you know
Are but simple expressions hackneyed,
But hell, what the hey;
Be different to dare!
Get your face out of your hair!
Do you mean what you say?
Or simply serve up, 'Hell to go!'
Or, 'Why me, don't ask?'
(Mean what I know?)
You lovers of the red hot last
Sit there over right
Out day and in day
As if the day of light
Had never seen you.
You say,
'We'll bridge that cross
When it comes to us.'
But it's never late than better

To burden up under the bear,
Before the feet of little pitter-patter
Comment to care
That your clichés are old
And your law of the letter dead,
Just as ice is cold.
The class of the head,
From time at day one,
Has taught this word infallible:
When your words are at a loss
And your sentences on the run,
It's time to bridge that cross
and work to try
A cliché reversible.

Daisy chains

John Whitworth, in his excellent book, *Writing Poetry*, talks about a form of writing called a Daisy chain.[4] The idea is that the last letter of each word is the same as the first letter of the following word. Whitworth gives some examples of daisy-chain poems, but suggests that to do this with rhyme and regular metre would be nearly impossible.[5] Of course, that was meant as a challenge. Following is an attempt at a rhymed and metred daisy chain. By the way, Whitworth didn't say the poems had to make sense!

Effervescent trunculating Gnomes

Effervescent trunculating Gnomes
Stand daring ghostly yuletide Ewes,
So opulent their reticulated domes;
Some even notice Ebert tango ontop pews.

4 John Whitworth. *Writing Poetry*, 2nd ed. (London: A & C Black, 2006). First edition, 2001.
5 This comment was not included in the 2nd edition, so I suspect he was inundated with examples from those who begged to differ!

Still, Leila and Derrida aptly yearn
New wisdom militant too often near,
Reluctant to open Nirvana's stringent turn,
Now will languish hope, eventless Seer.

Random motives stir Raifes slow, where
Earnest Trolls straddled dev'lish homes:
Startled Dwarves seek Kepler's secret there.
Effervescent trunculating Gnome.

Here is an example from my friend, the fantasy writer Morton Benning. It actually sort of makes sense!

The Eight

The eight trolls survey yonder ridge, East turned,
Debating gems some elder rebel learned,
Denying goatish hapless siblings' snares,
Sneaks stalwart thief from milieu unawares.

Sans stolen Nordic children, ne'er returned,
Distress such heartsick kingdom malice earned,
Did dispatch hero over river road,
Descent to oust the eldritch halfwit toads.

Sung gallant tune encouraging god's storm,
Mjolnir resounding, glowing godchief form.
Met trollish hoods still lounging gapefaced, dumb,
Bombarded devils slain, num'rous succumb.

Below wan right the emasculated dregs,
Slow, watchful, lest this saboteur reneges
Sunrise entombing grievous sorrow wait,
Thenceforth haloed defenceless, stands stone eight.[6]

---

6 In Morton Benning, *The Tale of Alathymble Spaide and Other Such Nonsense* (Stone Table Books: Melbourne, 2018), 26f.

List poems

It is possible, and good fun, to produce an entire poem consisting of nothing other than a list. Choose a list of authors, sports stars, film actors, street names, cities, foods, plants, animals etc., and select a metre and rhyme pattern. See example of the list poem, *Poets, Novelists, Playwrights, Bards*, in chapter three. Here's another example, from *The Shaker Manifesto* of 1882, with an irregular metre.

The Shaker Abecedarius

Alligator, Beetle, Porcupine, Whale,
Bobolink, Panther, Dragonfly, Snail,
Crocodile, Monkey, Buffalo, Hare,
Dromedary, Leopard, Mud Turtle, Bear,
Elephant, Badger, Pelican, Ox,
Flying Fish, Reindeer, Anaconda, Fox,
Guinea Pig, Dolphin, Antelope, Goose,
Hummingbird, Weasel, Pickerel, Moose,
Ibex, Rhinoceros, Owl, Kangaroo,
Jackal, Opossum, Toad, Cockatoo,
Kingfisher, Peacock, Anteater, Bat,
Lizard, Ichneumon, Honeybee, Rat,
Mockingbird, Camel, Grasshopper, Mouse,
Nightingale, Spiker, Cuttlefish, Grouse,
Ocelot, Pheasant, Wolverine, Auk,
Periwinkle, Ermine, Katydid, Hawk,
Quail, Hippopotamus, Armadillo, Moth,
Rattlesnake, Lion, Woodpecker, Sloth,
Salamander, Goldfinch, Angleworm, Dog,
Tiger, Flamingo, Scorpion, Frog,
Unicorn, Ostrich, Nautilus, Mole,
Viper, Gorilla, Basilisk, Sole,
Whippoorwill, Beaver, Centipede, Fawn,
Xanthos, Canary, Polliwog, Swan,
Yellowhammer, Eagle, Hyena, Lark,
Zebra, Chameleon, Butterfly, Shark.

Palindromes

Palindromes are words or sentences that say the same thing when read backwards or forwards. Glenelg, a beachside suburb of Adelaide, is a palindrome as are 'civic' and 'race car.' One of the best know palindromic sentences is: A man! A plan! A Canal! Panama! For the brave at heart, attempt to produce a palindromic poem. It is possible. 'Weird Al' Yankovic did just that in his song *Bob*, composed entirely of palindromes collected from various sources.[7]

Bob

I, man, am regal - a German am I
Never odd or even
If I had a hi-fi
Madam, I'm Adam
Too hot to hoot
No lemons, no melon
Too bad I hid a boot
Lisa Bonet ate no basil
Warsaw was raw
Was it a car or a cat I saw?
Rise to vote, sir
Do geese see god?
'Do nine men interpret?' 'Nine men,' I nod
Rats live on no evil star
Won't lovers revolt now?
Race fast, safe car
Pa's a sap
Ma is as selfless as I am
May a moody baby doom a yam?
Ah, Satan sees Natasha
No devil lived on
Lonely Tylenol

7 'Weird Al' Yankovic. 'Bob', cited in *Genius*, http://genius.com/Weird-al-yankovic-bob-lyrics.

Not a banana baton
No 'x' in 'Nixon'
O, stone, be not so
O Geronimo, no minor ego
'Naomi,' I moan
'A Toyota's a Toyota'
A dog, a panic in a pagoda
Oh no! Don Ho!
Nurse, I spy gypsies – run!
Senile felines
Now I see bees I won
UFO tofu
We panic in a pew
Oozy rat in a sanitary zoo
God! A red nugget! A fat egg under a dog!
Go hang a salami, I'm a lasagna hog

Anagrams

You might also wish to try your hand at inventing your own poetic structure. Here's one I came up with, inspired by sestinas and my fascination with anagrams. It is built around various sets of four. The poem should have four stanzas of four lines each, with each line consisting of four feet (in any metre). The final word of each line must be formed from an anagram of a four letter word. The last word in each stanza becomes the first of the next stanza, with each subsequent end word dropping one line. Hence the end word pattern of 1-2-3-4; 4-1-2-3; 3-4-1-2; 2-3-4-1. It is a lot of structure for one poem, but that is part of the fun and the challenge. Here's an example inspired by the global financial crisis of 2008.

GFC

What childish dreams to love and live
in terraced homes far kept from evil
times. Yet no polished gloss can veil
an open fiscal rift so vile.

Enter the many men who vile
and vain trade human futures live
on line. They recollect no evil;
hide behind their corp'rate veil.

But then the monetary veil
falls, exposing untold vile
and well-rewarded deals that live
in boardrooms under lesser evil.

Under strain of A. Smith's evil
backs and banks break within veil
of hidden sub-prime deals that vile
sub-brokers sell. So shall recession live.

The examples of poems given in this chapter are in no danger of becoming classic poetry. But they do demonstrate the importance of understanding the complexity of words. A good poet makes words do what he or she wants them to do. And this takes practice.

CHAPTER 10:

Final Thoughts on Poetry

'Poetry seems to partake of the miraculous, as does all great art; it adds up to more than the sum of its parts.'

– Frances Stillman[1]

'Poetry enlarges the circumference of the imagination by replenishing it with thoughts of ever new delight, which have the power of attracting and assimilating to their own nature all other thoughts.'

– Percy Bysshe Shelley[2]

History, nature and future of poetry

Poetry, like clothing, goes through waves of fashion. At the moment, many lament the apparent low ebb of poetry. Some complain that only students of verse and other poets actually read contemporary poetry. It is almost impossible to publish poetry collections unless one self-publishes – and is willing to pass on cartons of unsold books to one's heirs. Others are less pessimistic. They believe there is something fundamental about poetry that cannot be lost or abandoned. Certain forms of poetry may come in and out of fashion, and we may need to look in some unexpected places to find poetry, but as long as literate societies exist, so too will poetry.

Some years ago I was in Iran for a conference in Tehran. At the same time their national book fair was being held, so I thought I would use a free afternoon to go and take a look. I was surprised to discover that poetry outsold prose fiction! And in the beautiful city of Estefan in central Iran people gather on weekend evenings along the linear parks on either side of the picturesque river flowing through the city to listen to Farsi poetry being recited, both classic and contemporary. I was expecting crowds of some dozens, or perhaps hundreds, but the usual numbers,

1 Frances Stillman, *The Poet's Manual and Rhyming Dictionary*, vii.

2 P.B. Shelley, 'A Defense of Poetry' in *Essays, Letters from Abroad. Translations and Fragments from P. B. Shelley*, ed. Mary Shelley (Edward Moxon: London, 1840).

spread between various popular gathering points, averages 20 000 to 30 000 – each weekend. So there is hope for poetry!

But poetry will not make a resurgence unless it has knowledgeable readers. To achieve this poetry needs to be taught again in our schools. Sadly, too few teachers today understand the basics of poetry. This means that all that most students are ever exposed to is the writing of a few Haikus and a bit of free verse, both of which are often poorly understood. So when they come across a clever, quality poem later in life, they are unlikely to be able to appreciate it.

In India, cricket is a multi-million dollar sport followed by nearly the entire population. Children learn to play the game from a young age and understand its intricacies. A twenty-twenty match (a fast-paced modern version of the game) will be watched and cheered on by tens of thousands of spectators. But if the same match were held in America and free tickets given out, few would attend, and most of those would sit in perplexed silence. Cricket could never be marketed to the US unless young people learn to play the game. Yet we wait and hope for a resurgence of poetry in modern English-speaking society while doing little to teach its beauty and nuances to children and youth.

The great poets of the late nineteenth and early to mid-twentieth century would struggle to be published today. And if published, few would read or appreciate what they had achieved. The tragedy is that those today with the talent to produce quality poetry often never develop this talent fully, seldom invest the time to produce great poems, and when they do, it's mainly for the enjoyment of a few close friends who have the background to appreciate what has been achieved. But this can all change if the art of poetry is rediscovered, if educators are taught the basics of the art so they can pass on to their students at least a rudimentary appreciation of quality poetry.

Yet despite all the handicaps, poetry continues to find its own life and its own new forms of expression, whether in hip-hop lyrics or the continued growth of performance poetry and poetry slams in which the emphasis is on the dynamic, entertaining and sometimes confronting 'reading' or recitation of poetry.

The following syllabic poem is my own reflection on the nature and future of poetry. It was written as the final assignment for a university poetry class over thirty years ago, when not many outside the American inner cities had heard of rap. It was written at a time when the future of poetry seemed particularly bleak. It was written at a time when older poets and readers of poetry could still remember when great poets produced collections of poems that sold well and were widely read and recited. But those days had passed and some wondered whether there was any commercially viable future for quality poetry. The poem expresses the view that there is something basic and primordial about poetry that can never be lost from human experience.

The Poetic Circle

In the beginning, darkness and silence.
      Then from darkness arose
a lonely walking through the primal sward,
      speaking innocence
      and a simple mimic that
      some laureate like Lord
Tennyson

might have called onomatopoetic.
      Then mimic and music
danced together like animals in heat,
      waiting orgasmic
      merging of primord'al sound
      and proto-rhythmic bleat-
ing beating

beat of hollowed log and stretched-skin drum. Sound
      and beat conceived, and bore
a towering, swinging, singing offspring
      dancing round and round
      the ancient campfire burning,
      with blood-stained victors chanting
the story

of their triumphal hunt. The stalk, the kill,
    the words, the beat can scarce
remember how to live in this deso-
    late landscape of will
    and passion. They drift along,
    like extinct buffalo,
walking ghosts

grazing sand-swept desert rivers. In time
    the rhythmic beat became
iambic metre, waltzing gently 'cross
    each measured, light rhyme
    verse. But those modern bards sang
    of falling rain, and loss
of a girl

named Caroline, they might have courted once.
    The age old savage beat
was seasoned now with mince and melody;
    the fine opulence
    of inverted metaphor –
    of rhyme and simile.
Device was

crafted to device and fine ceramic
    form, 'til last we reached lin-
guistic climax with Chaucer's Saxon-French-
    Indo-Europic
    English language. Charlie Brown
    believes we might have glimpsed
poetry.

But Schroeder abhors structure as stifling
    of creative freedom
and supports *vers libre* and the prose *trouvere*.
    With Snoopy being

unwilling or unable
to resolve the matter,
each poet's

left to write what seems most inimical
before the reflection
of a million blank faces that resist
the postmodern call
for Hermes' abdication.
Wordmongers now desist.
Construction

has once more ceased on the tow'r in Babel,
three lines short of heaven
this time. Again chaotic rhapsody
and laughing rubble
are all that remain of that
proud spire since poetry
chose to fall

on her own sword. I might've thought her dead,
were it not for the beat
I heard wafting o'er the ghetto today.
It resonated
with a proto-rhythmic bleat-
ing beating beat, the way
sound echoes

through a hollowed log, or maybe like some
youth, rapping out his dreams
on rusting, back street rubbish bin. He sang,
but his primal song
was not about Caroline –
but his own death. It rang
through the streets;

a squalling orphan ransomed C-section,
    and left my soul feeling
oddly at home in that urban jungle.
    In celebration
    of my discovery, I
    endeavoured to mumble
Some lofty

apropos words– but they were mutely lost
    in the primal strain. Then
I tried to quote a line in the stillness
    from Browning or Frost
    to suit the occasion. But
    there was only darkness –
and silence.

Some final advice on writing poetry

- Write down words, phrases and sounds that catch your imagination or strike you as interesting. Play around with them in your head and on paper. Is there the seed of a poem in them?
- Pick a simple or even complex form and try to write a poem in that pattern.
- Not everything you write needs to be read by or shown to anyone else. You will be afraid to write down anything unless it's perfect from the beginning. Your notebook is your own 'safe place' to play with words and ideas. Most will amount to nothing, but some will grow into poems that you will want to share.
- Use tools like a thesaurus and rhyming dictionary. It's not cheating!
- Send your best efforts off to small literary magazines, websites and competitions – even church newsletters. Eventually, you'll get something published.
- Read books of poetry that you enjoy for inspiration. Good poets buy and read poetry!

- If you're finding it hard to write poetry, try some stream of consciousness or free verse. You could even write about how hard it is to write poetry at the moment. This can often get you moving, and some of what is produced in such exercises can be surprisingly powerful.
- Write the kind of poetry you enjoy reading, not what you think others want to hear. You can then at least be assured that there is one person who likes your poem!

I'll let Shelley have the last word on poetry.

> 'Poetry is indeed something divine. It is at once the centre and circumference of knowledge.... It is at the same time the root and blossom of all other systems of thought; it is that from which all spring, and that which adorns all; and that which, if blighted, denies the fruit and the seed, and withholds from the barren world the nourishment and succession of the scions of the tree of life.'[3]

3 Percy Bysshe Shelley, *A Defence of Poetry*, 101.

Writing Prose

Chapter 11:

The Emerging World of Christian Fiction

> *'The days are past when anyone – writer, editor, or publisher – need apologize for producing a Christian novel. In fact, Christian fiction is widely recognized as the Cinderella of publishing. It has outgrown its former status as a mere publishing genre or subcategory to become a full-fledged market segment with dozens of its own genres.'*
>
> – Ron Benrey[1]

Fiction is generally understood as prose works dealing with imagined characters and events. Within this broad category, Christian fiction occupies a growing niche, but is far from a new phenomenon. John Bunyan wrote Christian fiction in the seventeenth century. In the nineteenth century George MacDonald, one of the founders of the modern fantasy genre, wrote Christian fiction. C.S. Lewis, who wrote *The Chronicles of Narnia* and a sci-fi trilogy, remains one of the most successful fiction writers of all time – and he did it writing fiction with clear and intentional Christian themes. So when we hear today about the emergence of Christian fiction we might well wonder what's new. Christian fiction, in one form or another, has been around for a very long time. What is different is the number of writers now producing explicitly Christian fiction, and the marketing of these books to a targeted Christian audience.

When I was a teenager in the 1970s Christian bookstores were fairly small shops that sold Bibles (King James versions for the adults and NIVs for the youth), Sunday School and Holiday Bible Adventure material, and 'Jesus loves you' pencils and stickers. Christian bookstores nowadays still carry these traditional items, albeit with much greater variety, but they also have some very new features, including such things as children's playgrounds, coffee shops and CD and DVD rooms. And they have something else that was unheard of in the 1970s – dedicated fiction sections which often comprise several rows of shelving.

---

1 Ron Benrey, *Writing Christian Fiction* (New York: Alpha, 2007). xxii.

Christian fiction, especially in the US, has become a mass movement of writers and readers with dedicated publishers and a retail network of Christian bookstores stocking and selling the work of Christian representatives of almost every genre; including Christian romance, sci-fi, fantasy, crime novels, and historical fiction. Once I even met a writer whose proclaimed genre was Christian erotica – though I have doubts about how well this will catch on at my local Christian bookstore!

The point, of course, is that for a variety of reasons, there has been a surge in the production and marketing of a range of Christian fiction genres paralleling the emergence of Christian music some decades earlier, in which virtually every style of music had its specifically Christian representatives. As with the Christian music scene, this has had both benefits and drawbacks. On the plus side, it is now much easier to get stories published that deal positively with faith issues. Christian readers who may have shied away from many mainstream genres now have a greater diversity of Christian literature from which to choose. On the downside, there is a risk of adding to the ghettoisation of Christianity, with Christians only reading Christian versions of their favourite genres.

There is also the risk that many good Christian writers and their works will be labelled as 'Christian' for marketing purposes, and not gain exposure through mainstream publishers and bookshops. The Christian community can all too easily end up writing only for ourselves. This is a far cry from the situation of those early writers of Christian fiction, who wrote books that would appeal also to a mainstream market. These days, as soon as an author presents a work with strong Christian themes, regardless of how well written it is, the mainstream publisher will pass it on to their religious label to be marketed through the Christian bookstore network. This not only puts pressure on authors of Christian fiction to write within a much narrower band of interest, but it greatly diminishes the reach of contemporary writers of Christian fiction, compared to what authors like C.S. Lewis were able to achieve. Lewis' work, of course, was exceptional. But in the current climate, no mainstream publisher would have taken on *The Lion, The Witch and the Wardrobe*. This would have been sent straight to one of the religious presses, to be promoted exclusively within the Christian market.

A few years ago I was asked by a Christian publisher if I would like to serve as the founding editor of a new fantasy imprint that would publish a mix of mainstream and Christian titles. It was a great opportunity. It would be a chance to help get some good new writers established and to gain a better foothold for Christian fiction among mainstream titles. I knew the task would be challenging, but I must admit that my previous experiences on editorial advisory boards had done little to prepare me for the world of publishing. Nonetheless, with the necessary mix of boldness and naiveté required for such ventures, *Stone Table Books* was born. Three years, two dozen titles, and a change of parent companies later, I am still only beginning to understand the complexity and ever-changing world of contemporary publishing.

But those observations can wait for a later chapter. What is important here is what I have learned about the world of Christian fiction. It is a niche market, which should simplify some things. But it is not always an easy market to write for or to publish within. Firstly, any books that have too obvious a Christian theme are near impossible to get into mainstream bookstores, or to get reviewed outside of Christian periodicals and websites. But if the book is not overtly Christian enough, or contains ideas and themes that may challenge some people's thinking (which good literature is supposed to do), then it is hard to get the book into Christian bookstores. A niche market can be difficult to break into, but if that market is itself divided into competing and often non-cooperating sub-groups, the task becomes even more challenging.

For writers based outside of the US, getting published by a US Christian publisher is difficult – though not impossible. The writer soon discovers not only that they are asked to align their spelling and grammar with US norms (which is fair enough) but there are a host of 'don'ts' and 'no go' areas that are often quite strictly enforced. Ron Benrey, in his book *Writing Christian Fiction*, goes through the list that many US-based publishers of Christian fiction expect. These include, as Ron Benrey explains, 'conservative Christian values, Christian characters who don't drink alcoholic beverages, play cards, dance or gamble, no profanity, no strong violence, no overt sexuality, and chaste relationships that downplay the physical component of love.'[2] For some US Christian publishers and booksellers, there is a view that Christian fiction must portray the conversion of one of the main characters, or at the very least their return to an active life of faith and church attendance, as if these are the only themes worthy of the attention of Christian writers and readers. Some writers may find they are not comfortable making this level of change to their story, or avoiding the tough issues that motivated them to write the story in the first place. Other writers might feel that the writing has been reduced to a formula, and they are simply being asked to produce slightly different versions of the same story. While the emergence of small independent presses and self-publishing have helped Christian writers in the US and elsewhere be more diverse in their creativity, the reality is that those who choose these routes seldom sell more than a couple hundred copies of their books.

The US Christian fiction publishing scene has a huge influence. US trends continue to have a major impact on Christian fiction in the rest of the English-speaking world. It is a tricky market to work with, especially for writers not based in the US. The good news is that there is a large and growing market for Christian fiction, albeit dominated by the US market. And it is possible to break into this market and work with it, even for writers not based in the US. But if you want to publish in the US Christian fiction market, you must do your homework and be willing to adapt to a range of both written and unwritten conventions and expectations.

Exercise: Faith in fiction

Choose a favourite fiction genre, e.g., romance or fantasy. Write a 1000 word short story in that genre that has a strong Christian element. This can be done by having a Christian character or characters, by portraying a distinctive Christian theme, such as forgiveness or sacrificial death for others, by using a Christian setting such as a worship service, church group or monastic community, having the protagonist experience the help or intervention of God, or perhaps some combination of these. Be faithful to both your chosen genre and the faith message or image you are seeking to convey.

---

2 Ron Benrey, *The Complete Idiot's Guide to Writing Christian Fiction* (New York: Alpha, 2007), 5.

CHAPTER 12:

Form, Genre and Audience

> *'This book is a classic of the singular contemporary romance genre. There is sex and murder. Features thrilling adventures. Much sophisticated, top-notch romance. Set in land-locked Burundi. Has poetry and prose, myths and legends. Has extraordinary talents. Has everything.'*
>
> – letter to a publisher from an aspiring author[1]

Fiction is a very broad category. It can be broken up into forms like the novella or the short story based largely on the size of the work, or divided into genre categories such as romance, fantasy or crime thriller. It can also be looked at in terms of audience, especially if this is age-based (such as young adult). For the author setting out to write a fictional tale, some important questions need to be decided before the first keystroke is made.

Forms of fiction

Flash fiction. These are very short stories, usually well under 1000 words. A number of competitions and outlets for flash fiction, especially online, have arisen in recent years as the form grows in popularity. While the term flash fiction is relatively new, such stories have long had a niche, and in earlier years were often designated as 'short, short stories'. Flash fiction will normally contain all or most of the elements of the short story, but everything is more condensed, faster paced, and often much remains hinted at rather than explicitly narrated.

Short story. The short story is a self-contained piece of prose fiction that is generally not subject to such things as chapter divisions, and normally is well under 10 000 words in length. It often deals with a single character, scene or episode as the format does not allow for complex development and multiple plot lines. Most good fiction writers learned their craft by

1 Cited in Sammy Looker, *Something Nasty in the Slushpile. How not to get published* (London: Constable, 2014), 68.

writing short stories, and many successful novelists continue to write short stories, even though they are seldom commercially successful.

Novella. The novella is more sustained than a short story, and usually has a more complex storyline. It may well have chapter divisions and will often run from 10 000 to 30 000 words, though no agreed definition of length exists. The name itself simply means 'little novel' and this is precisely what the novella is. There is a wide gulf between the short story and the novel in terms of length, and the amount of character and plot development possible within the two forms. The novella occupies a middle ground between these. Ideally, the novella should be designed and written as such, and not simply be a short story that got out of hand, or a novel that ran out of steam. Unlike the short story, the novella normally covers more than a single incident and has a clear development of plot and characters.

Unlike the novel, the novella has one or at most a few main characters, a relatively simple plot with fewer conflicts to be resolved, and often revolves around a single significant event or situation. There are generally no subplots. As most novellas are stand alone works, there are no cliff-hangers, and no endings that leave themselves open for a sequel. The storyline of the novella, while more complex than that of a short story, should be compact and complete within itself. Novellas are also works of fiction. A short biography is not a novella, but simply a short biography. Novellas are also generally written for adults. A short Young Adult novel is generally not considered a novella simply because it is less than 30 000 words in length. George Eliot's *Silas Marner* (1861), Franz Kafka's *Metamorphosis* (1915), C.S. Lewis' *The Great Divorce* (1945), George Orwell's *Animal Farm* (1945), Ernest Hemingway's *The Old Man and the Sea* (1952), Richard Bach's *Jonathan Livingstone Seagull* (1970) and Paul Coelho's *The Alchemist* (1988) are good examples of novellas.

Novel. The most common form of prose fiction today is indisputably the novel. Developed in Elizabethan England, the form has steadily evolved to the size, range and style of book-length works we encounter around the world today. Many novels are single, easy to manage volumes. But some extend to quite massive tomes, such as Tolstoy's *War and Peace* and Tolkien's *The Lord of the Rings*. Yet most people have a fairly clear idea of what a novel is. They might struggle to define the concept, but they know a novel when they see one.

Play/screenplay. The screenplay, one might argue, is a far more popular literary form today than the novel. But, taken as a piece of literature to be read, few apart from directors and actors actually read screenplays. Even the stage play, with a far smaller audience in mind, is more often read as literature (e.g., the plays of Shakespeare, Ben Jonson or Oscar Wilde) than their screenplay counterparts. Both forms consist almost entirely of dialogue, with the occasional note indicating something about the setting or tone of the conversation. The descriptions of scenes, characters and even the manner in which the dialogue is delivered are generally left to the director and actors to bring to life. As literature, therefore, these works may seem somewhat 'incomplete'. Nonetheless, some of the better stage plays have become classic works of literature in their own right. While most readers do not read screenplays, a recent exception has been J.K. Rowling's *The Cursed Child*,[2] which continues the Harry Potter and Hogwarts story to the next generation. Large numbers of the script were sold and read by Harry Potter fans unwilling to wait for the play, and even longer for the film.

The *verse novel*. Long before the rise of the novel, longer tales were usually narrated in verse form. This was the case from Homer through to Milton's *Paradise Lost*. In recent years there has been a resurgence of telling longer stories in verse. These mostly occur in some form of free verse. The range of what is possible in a verse novel is illustrated by my former student and friend, Valerie Volk. Her short verse novel *A Promise of Peaches* (Ginninderra Press, 2011) tells the story of a post-war immigrant family to Australia. She followed this up with her massive, and masterful, *Passion Play: The Oberammergau Tales* (Wakefield Press, 2013), which is a modern version of the Canterbury Tales in which the pilgrims are all on a bus trip to attend the famous Oberammergau passion play in Southern Bavaria. While verse novels are appearing more frequently, they are usually designed for a smaller 'art house' audience than for the mass market.

---

2 J.K. Rowling, John Tiffany and Jack Thorne (London: Sphere, 2017).

Genres

Most readers (and writers) do not choose their preferred fiction so much by its form or length as by its genre. Genre, to be sure, is a slippery word in literary circles. Broadly, it is used to designate the kind of fiction one is dealing with. It should be kept in mind that each of the following general categories of genre can also be divided into a number of sub-genres

Historical fiction. These are works of fiction set in a concrete historical period other than the present or very recent past. They are often based upon actual characters and events. Writers of historical fiction must also be keen amateur historians and capable of researching the period and place in which their story is set.

Speculative fiction. This is a broad category that covers any fiction in which the world in which the story takes place, or parts of that world, are created by the author. Hence the author is 'speculating' about a possible reality rather than setting the story in the so-called 'real' world. This could be as major as the creation of a fictional planet or mythical world, as in many sci-fi and fantasy novels, or as subtle as a world in which someone has some special magical ability, as is the case in *magical realism,* or in which some other aspect of reality has been altered. Or it could involve a setting which explores aspects of the afterlife or even spiritual realities. The broader category of speculative fiction is often used to describe those works which do not easily fit in the categories of fantasy or science-fiction, but which nevertheless are clearly not set in our ordinary world or reality.

Fantasy. Modern fantasy, having begun in Victorian England, is generally characterised by the creation of an imaginary world inhabited by special kinds of creatures, often drawn from classical and Northern mythology, and making use of magic. While 'classical' fantasy, in the vein of writers like Tolkien and Ursula Le Guin, tends to have a medieval feel to it and focuses largely on human or human-like characters, there is also fantasy in which all the characters are animals, for instance Brian Jacques' *Redwall* series; and nonsense fantasy, such as Lewis Carroll's Alice books or Roald Dahl's *Willy Wonka and the Chocolate Factory*.

Science-fiction. Modern science-fiction traces its popular origins to the works of Jules Verne (1828-1905) and H.G. Wells (1866-1946). It is closely related to fantasy and was originally seen as part of the same genre. The chief differences between fantasy and science-fiction is that the imaginary worlds of sci-fi are usually other planets or set in Earth's future; and in place of magic, advanced technology is relied upon to explain how and why extraordinary things happen. The typical medieval feel of the fantasy story is replaced by a more futurist and technology-dependent world in science-fiction.

Thriller. Broadly, anything that keeps us on the edge of our seats might be described as a thriller. Usually these are political, medical, espionage or terrorist focused works in which life and death depend upon the ability of the protagonist(s) to solve the mystery before it is too late. If too violent, frightening or macabre, however, the intended thriller can stray into the horror genre.

Horror. Stories meant simply to frighten or scare the reader, through either plenty of blood and gore, continually heightened suspense, and/or grotesque monsters or figures such as werewolves and vampires, are generally classified as horror – though it should be noted that some recent vampire and werewolf stories are actually more teen romance than horror. The contemporary horror genre has its antecedents in Victorian literature, especially Mary Shelley's *Frankenstein* (1818), Bram Stoker's *Dracula* (1897), Robert Louis Stevenson's *Dr. Jekyll and Mr. Hyde* (1886), and even in George McDonald's pre-Bram Stoker vampire story, *The Cruel Painter* (1874). This latter story by the pastor and spiritual writer helped inspire a group of writers I worked with to produce an anthology of modern Christian vampire stories.[3] The premise was that in a genre so dominated and obsessed with darkness, there must surely be a place for light.

Romance. When we think of romance the Mills and Boon books come immediately to mind. But romance as a genre is much broader than Mills and Boon, and Christian romance has particularly taken off in recent years. Romance novels are non- or mildly erotic love stories, usually written for a primarily female audience. The protagonists often have some obstacle to overcome (family, distance, jobs, health issues, etc.) in order

3 *Something in the Blood. Vampire Tales with a Christian Bite*, ed. M Worthing (Mosaic Press, 2015).

to be together. Romance novels sometimes struggle to gain full respect in the literary world. Yet they are very popular among readers and the genre is one of the most financially successful. Many contemporary romance novels are very well-written works which challenge the stereotype that adheres to this genre.

The Christian romance novel parallels its mainstream counterpart. One or both protagonists are Christian, and often it is faith-related issues that must be resolved in order to bring the couple together. Often, love cannot be found until one of the parties comes to faith, or turns back to the path of following God. In the US an entire sub-genre of Christian romance has emerged that might best be called ‘Amish romance’. In these stories the setting is usually the simple and often idealised Amish communities, with plenty of horses, buggies, ploughs, barn raisings, and community meals as the backdrop for the love story.

Crime. The crime genre is composed largely of the fictional ‘whodunit’ or detective story. The genre in its modern form was pioneered by writers like Arthur Conan Doyle with his Sherlock Holmes character. Also formative was Agatha Christie, one of the early, successful representatives of the genre. Those who write successfully in the crime genre often either have a legal or law enforcement background, or are very dedicated researchers.

A Christian influence can be brought into this genre through the use of religious characters. Good examples are G.K. Chesterton’s *Father Brown* stories and Ellis Peters with her *The Chronicles of Brother Cadfael* novels, set within a medieval English monastery. Each of these series of stories present an intelligent and amicable main character who is overtly committed to Christian ideals and a life of Christian service. While the crimes to be solved usually involve murder, there is opportunity to portray Christian characters in a more positive and complex light than often occurs in literature.

Humour. This genre is self-explanatory. Stories aimed to make us laugh are categorised as humour. These might range from spoofs of popular or respected works, satirical treatments of individuals or organisations, or simple slapstick. While much humorous writing is aimed at children and YA audiences, there is also room for humour in adult-oriented works. These are often combined with other genres, as for instance a vast number of romantic comedies, Terry Pratchett's fantasy *disk-world* novels, Douglas Adams' science-fiction *Hitchhikers' Guide to the Galaxy* series, or the non-fiction travel writing of Bill Bryson.

Literary. Increasingly, one reads of literary fiction as a 'genre.' Alternately, sometimes 'genre' writing is spoken of disparagingly, and the term 'literary' reserved for those books that are seen as rising above genre. Precisely what is meant by 'literary' is difficult to describe. Clearly all fiction is literary. But some works are written for a more literarily sophisticated audience, and the main feature of some works might seem to be their elegant literary style. Works classified as literary fiction often assume their readers are well-read, and appreciate the elegance of the prose as much as the story. While this category might seem the invention of booksellers more than writers or literature experts, it seems to have won a place among the categories of literary genres. Books such as Markus Zusak's *The Book Thief*, Carlos Ruiz Zafón's *The Shadow of the Wind*, Audrey Niffenegger's *The Time Traveler's Wife*, Yann Martel's *Life of Pi* and Nicholas Jose's *Paper Nautilus* have all, for good or ill, been classed as literary fiction. Yet what these works have in common, apart from being extremely well-written, hard to classify in some other genre, and unlikely to appeal to readers with who do not appreciate the beauty of language for its own sake, is difficult to say.

Children's and YA fiction. This is more of a category than a genre. Children's and young adult fiction comes in the same variety of genres as other literature. Also, whereas once the broad categories of children's or YA covered the field, we now speak of *middle grade readers* for 9-12 year olds, who set somewhere in between children's and YA, and *new adult,* for late teens and early 20s readers. A children's or YA book might be romance, crime, fantasy, humour, historical fiction, or any other genre that exists among adult literature. The only distinguishing feature of such books is that they are clearly written for younger readers and are usually marked by young characters, simpler vocabulary, less complex storylines and are usually of a shorter length than their adult-orientated counterparts.

For more information on children's and young adult writing, especially for books oriented to a Christian market and audience, see Rosanne Hawke's excellent introduction, *Riding the Wind: Writing for Children and Young Adults* (Morning Star, 2019).

The above survey is, of course, only a sampling of the ever-changing categories of genres. There are constantly new genres emerging, or being recognised. A few decades ago no one talked about steampunk, but we now recognise that it has its origins in late nineteenth-century science fiction and related genres. Stories set within computer-generated or virtual worlds, or cyber fiction, is a relatively new genre, not possible before the age of the computer. And there are endless possibilities for combining existing genres. If the story you want to write doesn't fit neatly into a particular genre, don't let that stop you from writing it. Who knows, it may turn out to be the first example of an entirely new genre or sub-genre.

Audience

Every writer should have in mind the kind of impact they want to have with the short story, novella or novel they are writing. This means they should also have an audience in mind. Identifying a specific group of readers will help with consistency and focus of writing.

As a writer, you might not put a great deal of thought into who your reading audience will be, but any potential publisher certainly will. If you're writing a query letter to a publisher, you should definitely include your intended or target audience. The mistake inexperienced writers often make is simply to say, 'I think this work will appeal to all readers', or words to similar effect. Generally, this simply shows that you haven't thought much about your target audience – and perhaps haven't written with one in mind. This could indicate a work that is stylistically and thematically all over the place. It might also mean that the work is so general in nature that it will be hard to market.

While all writers would like to think that every literate person would want to read their work, the reality is that each piece produced will have a restricted audience, determined by genre, theme, style and other considerations.

So give some thought to your target audience. Will they be predominantly male, female or mixed? Will they likely be blue collar or professional? Will they be university educated or not? Will they be younger adult, middle age or elderly? Are they likely to be Christian, Muslim, Buddhist, secular, or non-committed? Are they likely to be politically and culturally conservative or more moderate or liberal? While not all these questions will help you define your target audience, some of them will.

I find it helpful, once I have in mind a realistic target audience, to imagine a few representatives that I know from this group as I write. Some years ago I wrote a chess novel for middle grade readers.[4] I imagined the children I'd coached over the years and asked myself how they would respond to a particular scene, or what they might like to see happen next. If I could visualise them getting excited or laughing at a scene in the story, then I felt I was likely on the right track. If I couldn't imagine them being anything other than bored or confused as they plodded through to a more interesting section, then I knew I had more work to do.

Your story can and should be compelling. And it might head in unforeseen directions. But you neglect your target audience at your own peril.

4 The story of my chess novel is a sad and cautionary tale. I wrote it in the days before off-site computer back-ups. I had a completed draft of the novel on my laptop and had printed out a hard copy. I packed the hard copy with my laptop to take with me to a conference where I hoped to have some time in the evenings to do some final revisions. The laptop, along with my only hard copy, was stolen that very day from my office and the entire novel was lost. I never had the heart to start it over again. Lesson: always have back-ups for your back-ups of your creative work. And keep them up-to-date!

Chapter 13:

Characters, Point-of-View and Storyline

> *'It begins with a character, usually, and once he stands up on his feet and begins to move, all I can do is trot along behind him with a paper and pencil trying to keep up long enough to put down what he says and does.... I have very little to do... the characters themselves, they do what they do, not me.'*
>
> – William Faulkner[1]

A well-known saying is that the hardest and most important part of a thousand-mile journey is the first step. We might say something similar about writing a novel. The hardest and most important step is simply to begin writing, though that is more easily said than done. It takes some significant thought and planning.

Developing a project profile

Before beginning to write any new work an author will normally choose at least one from each of the following categories. This cross-section of Form, Genre, Function and Audience yields a basic project profile. Spend a bit of time thinking about how long of a piece you want to produce, what genre it will be, what impact you hope it will have on your readers, and, the point that many new writers often overlook, just what kind of reader do you imagine your story appealing to. For example, you may come up with one of the following profiles for the new work you are about to write:

Form:	Novel	[OR]	Novella
Genre:	Historical fiction		Romance
Function:	Entertain and enlighten		Inspire
Audience:	Christian and literary		Younger female

Avoid the trap of believing your story will appeal to everyone. One

1 William Faulkner, in *Faulkner at West Point*, ed. J. Fant and R. Ashley (Jackson, Miss: University Press of Mississippi, 2002), 101.

of the surest signs of an inexperienced writer is when they quickly respond to any question about who might buy and read their book with something like: 'Oh, there's something in here for everyone'; or 'This book will appeal to readers of all ages and backgrounds'; or 'I've given the manuscript to all my friends and family and everyone loved it.' If you write for everyone in general, you will likely end up appealing to no one in particular.[2]

Being clear about these points will help you stay focused as a writer. Of course, sometimes a story takes on a life of its own and goes in unintended directions. This may require some alterations, for the sake of consistency, to parts of the work already written. It is always much easier to adjust such things as your genre or target audience if you already had clear ideas about these from the beginning. While some writers explain that they felt like their story more or less wrote itself, clearly no story actually writes itself. That's what writers do. Sometimes we become so caught up in the world we have created that the way forward becomes clear, or as we imagine what our characters would say or do next. The story seems to simply progress in directions that we had not previously foreseen. But such experiences are ultimately the result of much thought and engagement with our characters within their world. It is still the writer at work, even when creative directions appear to arise from what is more sub-conscious than conscious reflection on the development of the story.

Storyline

What is the basic story you want to tell? While even a short story might have a few sub-plots running through it, every good piece of fiction will have a single, clear storyline. *The Lord of the Rings*, voted by readers in the English-speaking world as the most popular novel of the twentieth-century, contained a host of sub-plots. Would Aragorn become king?

---

2 By the same token, do not make your target audience unnecessarily small. A former colleague of mine who wrote theology books once submitted a manuscript to a publisher, who liked the book, and wrote back asking for a description of the intended target audience. My colleague replied that the book was aimed at conservative Christians who were well-read and had an open-minded view of the world. The publisher responded, somewhat tongue-in-cheek, that a dozen potential readers would not justify a print run!

Would Arwen forsake all to marry him? Would Saruman get his just deserts in the end? Would Merry and Pippin ever be reunited with the other hobbits? But the one overriding storyline that holds the trilogy together is the fate of the one ring and of Middle-earth. However interesting the many sub-stories running throughout the text, the main point of tension that kept the reader connected is the fate of the ring and the question of whether Frodo would somehow in the end manage to destroy it in the fires of Mount Doom. You may have a lot going on in your novel, but be clear in your own mind about the main storyline. Be careful not to depart from it for too long, and when you feel you must depart from it, make sure your excursus is ultimately connected to your main storyline.

If you are having difficulty determining what your main storyline is, ask yourself what is the point-of-tension or unresolved question that will keep the reader engaged to the very last page. A good story or novel will introduce early on some conflict that needs to be resolved, some mystery that needs to be unravelled, or hint at some dark secret that will make sense of the whole story. How the writer gradually works toward resolving or revealing this is another way of understanding what a storyline is and what it does.

Joseph Campbell and the Hero's Journey

You might decide to fall back on a tried-and-true narrative structure. The mythologist Joseph Campbell, in his book *The Hero with a Thousand Faces*,[3] identified what he believed was the essential plot outline that recurs in most great stories from classical mythology. In essence, he contended that it is the same story told over and over with new protagonists, obstacles and opponents. He called it the Hero's Journey. While the ten points of the storyline he identified reflect the great heroic tales of past ages, they also hold true for modern stories in which the hero might not be a warrior, but a young woman seeking her way in the world, and the danger not a dragon to be slain, but a difficult boss.

It is surprising how many stories fit unexpectedly well into this outline. I tried it with a novella I wrote called *The Winter Fae*. Even though I did not write the story with any thought of Campbell's outline in mind, it

3 Joseph Campbell. *The Hero with a Thousand Faces* (New York: Pantheon Books, 1949).

looks like I might well have used it as my narrative map. Campbell's ten storyline markers are given in italics.

The Hero's Journey and *The Winter Fae*[4]

1. *The ordinary world.* The story begins with 87-year-old Floyd, suffering from dementia, at home on his farm.
2. *The call to adventure*. Floyd begins to remember something he has forgotten: a childhood visit to Faerie. He is obsessed with making the journey into the Great Wood to find once more the woman he remembers as the Snow Mother
3. *Crossing the threshold.* Floyd walks through the back gate of his farm in the midst of a snow storm and ventures into the Great Wood. Whatever happens, he does not expect to return.
4. *Trials, friends and foes.* Floyd's children care about him but are worried by his increasing loss of memory. They want to put him in a nursing home. Floyd must go on his journey now, or forever miss the chance.
5. *Magical mentor.* After venturing deep into the Great Wood, Floyd encounters the Winter Fae, who saved him once before when he was a child and who he remembered as the Snow Mother. It is the job of the Winter Fae to watch over fairy children as their parents sleep through the winter.
6. *The dragon's lair.* While there is much good in Faerie, there is also a growing shadow cast by the Tamarack, a malevolent tree sprite who is seeking to destroy Floyd and is a threat to Faerie. Eventually, Floyd must venture back into the Great Wood alone to confront the Tamarack.
7. *Moment of despair.* Floyd realises that he cannot remain in Faerie. He is encouraged by the Winter Fae to return home to his farm, reinvigorated, and live out his remaining years in peace. But this would mean leaving the children of Faerie in peril.
8. *Ultimate treasure/defeat of the dragon.* Floyd risks everything and

4 M. Worthing. *The Winter Fae. A Fantasy Novella* (Melbourne: Stone Table Books, 2018).

defeats the Tamarack, but at the cost of his own life.

9. *Homeward bound.* Floyd's homeward journey takes place without him. His body is found and his children grieve his death, but Floyd also leaves them with a mystery.
10. *Rebirth and the champion's return.* While Floyd's body has been found, his spirit has been set free from the ravages of age and dementia. He awakens to find himself in a heaven-like setting, where his wife and many others are waiting for him.

If I had written the novella with the Hero's Journey outline in mind, I wonder whether the story would have been easier to write, or clearer in its development. I find it interesting that in those places where I seem to depart from the path of the Hero's Journey, there was still something there. Floyd doesn't, for instance, literally make it home again, but his body does, and his spirit also finds its home. Also, in my story I inverted the dragon's lair (6) and the moment of despair (7), but they seemed to work just as well, and both elements are still clearly present.[5]

Exercise: Finding your hero's journey

Set the Hero's Journey outline against a novel you have written, or one you are working on or thinking of writing. Map it out as I did with my novella, *The Winter Fae*. To what extent are the basic elements of the Hero's Journey present in your story? Is anything missing? An awareness of this basic narrative structure, which appears embedded in our human story-telling psyche, may well give your own storyline greater clarity and direction.

5 Christopher Vogler has adapted Campbell's basic structure for writers in his book, *The Writer's Journey: Mythic Structure for Writers* (Seattle: Michael Wiese, 2007), and previously, *The Writer's Journey: Mythic Structure for Storytellers and Screenwriters* (Seattle: Michael Wiese, 1992). If Campbell's structure interests you as a writer, one of Vogler's books should be on your reading list.

The Messianic Hero

There are a number of recurrent storylines in literature.[6] One that deserves mention alongside that of the hero's journey is largely inspired by the Gospels and the impact they have had upon generations of readers. It is the tale of the messianic hero. The outline of these stories generally runs as follows:

1. A person, group, city or all of humanity are in great danger.
2. A mysterious figure appears from outside the group with special abilities and/or powers.
3. The messiah figure agrees or decides to rescue those who cannot rescue themselves.
4. The group/city/world is saved, but the messiah figure either dies in the process, or makes a great personal sacrifice.
5. The rescued group is somehow changed by the hero's sacrifice. They not only survive, but will now live better, more meaningful lives.

The story of the messianic hero can be found in one variation or another in most superhero stories and in many sci-fi stories. Classic examples include the *Superman* cycle of stories, or the figure of Neo in the *Matrix* trilogy.[7]

Main character(s)

Who are your main characters going to be? How will they be interesting, engaging and believable? What is their backstory? Good writers spend much time thinking about what their main characters are like before they begin to flesh them out in their text. You might only include hints of this backstory in your writing, but if you have imagined something about the history, tastes, habits, passions, political views, education, failures and fears of your main characters, then you will be able to have them

6 See for instance Christopher Booker, *The Seven Basic Plots: Why We Tell Stories* (London: Bloomsbury, 2017). Booker argues that there are only seven basic plots in all of literature, and these are: 1. Overcoming the monster, 2. Rags to riches, 3. The Quest, 4. Voyage and Return, 5. Rebirth, 6. Comedy, and 7. Tragedy.

7 Cf. M. Worthing, *The Matrix Revealed. The Theology of the Matrix Trilogy* (Adelaide: Pantaenus Press, 2004).

respond to situations in ways that are consistent and believable.[8] Some writers actually write scenes and dialogue for their characters that they have no intention of including in their final draft simply as an exercise for exploring the characters' personalities and responses to a range of situations. Actors often do something similar with the characters they play, putting them into situations that do not actually appear in the script in order to gain a better feel for the character. While readers are unlikely to pick up directly on the background work that has gone into your characters, they will have a sense as to whether the characters are real and believable. Characters in stories who suddenly do random or unexpected things without explanation are frustrating to the reader and are the sign of a writer who has not put sufficient thought into his or her characters apart from the actual scenes in which they appear.

To help you think about your characters, make a list of them and briefly describe their appearance, vital stats, and personality.[9] Ask yourself whether these traits actually go together. For instance, is your molecular biologist also a weekend prize fighter, or your egocentric business climber an active member of the RSPCA? Would your farm hand show up at a night club at all, let alone wearing an Armani suit, and is your petite Sunday School teaching mother of four likely to drive a V-8 ute? If these combinations seem just a bit too unlikely, such things will also strike your readers as odd. Of course, by all means, the writer should not shy away from challenging stereotypes, but this should always be done with intentionality and in a way that is consistent with your character's profile.

Give careful attention to your characters' names. The name should fit the personality. You don't want an evil or sinister character with a name like Justin Goodwood or Charity Lovelace, nor kind and sympathetic characters with names like Jezebel and Bruno. A computer geek would not likely be nicknamed Ruggers and the captain of the footy team would not likely be called Spock by his friends. Also, avoid giving your main character names that sound too much alike. I received an otherwise very good story once

---

8 Cf. Lisa Cron, *Story Genius: How to Use Brain Science to Go Beyond Outline and Write a Riveting Novel* (Ten Speed Press, 2016) who urges writers to consider what turning points in a character's background have made them who they are, and what misconceptions they have about people and the world around them that will be challenged in the narrative.

9 Caz Williams, a writer and theatre person in my writing group, says she likes to have her characters empty their pockets and see what is in them and why. Anything that can get you thinking creatively about who your characters are is a useful tool to employ.

in which the main characters were named Kathrine, Kenneth and Katie. All began with the same sound, all were two syllables and all were very Anglo. Things were especially confusing in the story's dialogue, and even the writer in a few places had clearly confused the names.

So where does one find good names? The best place to search for given names is in a good baby name book. Every writer should have one by their desk. Read through the names, making a shortlist of those that might suit your character. Let the list set for a day or two, then come back and see which one or ones stand out. For family names there is no better source than your local phonebook (old copies of these can still be found lying around) or internet directory. There are also online sites that provide lists of popular names by country and also by era. These are very useful for authentic sounding names of characters from specific cultures or times. You cannot make up better, and often quirkier names, than the ones worn every day by real people.

Choosing good names for your character might sound easy, but it is not. Even experienced writers struggle with this. John Marsden, for instance, confesses that:

> Choosing names is one of the things I find hardest about writing. Among the reference books beside me when I write are a dictionary of surnames, a dictionary of first names, some old class rolls, a telephone directory, a postcode book, and a dictionary of mythology. I dip into them all the time for names of people and places, but even with their help it can take hours to get the right ones.[10]

A good character, of course, is more than a good name. A good character is interesting and believable. The reader will care about what happens to them, even if this means that they hope they 'get what's coming to them' in the end. They will be complex. The 'good' characters will have faults, and the 'bad' characters, or the antagonists, will not be irredeemable. Your main character or characters will carry your storyline. Your minor characters will do their job in the narrative and not try to steal the show. As one writer put it; 'If they are minor characters, they've got to advance the storyline or twist it or relieve tension or convey information – and then they've got to get out of the way.'[11]

10 John Marsden. *Everything I Know about Writing* (Sydney: Pan Macmillan, 2004), 99.

11 Orson Scott Card, *Characters and Viewpoint* (Cincinnati: Writers Digest Books, 2010), 19.

Exercise: Character sketch

Choose an interesting person you know and ask to interview them. Make notes on their life history, their likes and dislikes, their general demeanor and personality. Then write a brief story or scene from a story (300-400 words) in which a fictionalised version of your interviewee appears. Remember to change the name and any other identifying details. The purpose of the exercise is to learn to draw upon your contacts with real-life characters in order to create believable characters for your fiction. This is a technique used even by highly skilled and experienced writers. J.R.R. Tolkien, for instance, used his friend C.S. Lewis as a model for his character Treebeard. Of course, Lewis looked nothing like Treebeard, but Tolkien imagined the way Lewis might think, talk, etc. to lend reality to his personification of the leader of the Ents.

Voice and point of view

Very early in the writing process, sometimes even before the first sentence of your novel is written, you will need to make some decisions about the voice and point of view of your story. While these might need to be changed later if what you are doing is not working, it's difficult to start writing a story without some of these basic decisions at least tentatively in place. Who, for instance, is telling the story? And from whose perspective will the story be told? Will your story be told in the first, second or third person – or in some complex combination of these? You might choose to tell your story in the 'I' and 'we' language of a person or persons who are a part of the events narrated. In this case, who will tell the story? It does not have to be the main character. You might – and this is quite difficult and rare – choose to tell your story in 'you' language, narrated by someone telling another person what they (the reader or hearer) did or will do. More commonly, a story is told in the third person language of 'he', 'she' and 'they' by a narrator. But even an unnamed narrator will have a point of view.

In addition to the basic decision about first, second or third person language, the writer needs to think about the perspective or stance of their storyteller. For instance, a third-person account may be in the voice of an omniscient and neutral narrator, or a narrator who only knows what he or she has been told by those involved. Today, people often speak in terms such as deep POV and close third-person POV to indicate the range and significance of the possible points of view from which your story might be told. A simple third-person narrator, for instance, will not be omniscient. They only know the part of the story they have seen or heard. A close third-person POV will be more than a mere observer, but someone deeply connected to the main character(s) and their fate. A narrator who has a vested interest in the story will be inclined to either defend or judge the actions of the characters. In all of these cases the narrator inevitably follows a particular point of view, that is to say, they see and tell the story from the perspective of one character or group of characters. Also, an all-seeing narrator does not have to remain anonymous and behind the scenes. In Markus Zuzak's *The Book Thief*, Death is the narrator. He sees all, but is not neutral. Nor does he remain silent regarding his own opinions. He sees and tells the story from the perspective of the girl, Liesel, whose friends and family he visits all too frequently. This is his point of view.

If you choose the more personal approach of a first-person account, you must decide which of your characters will tell the story, and also why they are telling the story. If the main character in your story arrives on the scene after the beginning, or dies before the end, choosing the voice of a secondary character may be a better option.

Once you find a point of view that works for your story, stick with it. Many beginning writers shift their point of view within the story – and sometimes even within the same sentence – without any apparent awareness they are doing so. Sometimes shifting the point of view from once character to another can be used to good effect, as for instance when two different parts of the story are being brought together, or when we need to see the action from more than one point of view.[12] When this is done, often the viewpoint switch takes place with alternating chapters,

12 An excellent example of this is to be found in Wendy Noble's *Beast-Speaker* trilogy (Melbourne: Stone Table Books, 2017-2019) in which the POV switches regularly to that of a secondary character to give the reader insights and a perspective that cannot be gained from the main character.

and is clearly indicated. Jumping from one person's point of view to another within the same chapter or section, with no clear explanation or indication, is sometimes called 'head hopping.' Ursula Le Guin, author of the popular *Earthsea* series, put it well when she wrote: "In fiction, inconsistent point of view is a very frequent problem. Unless handled with awareness or skill, frequent point of view shifts jerk the reader around, bouncing in and out of incompatible identifications, confusing emotion, garbling the story."[13]

Exercise: Changing voice

Choose a scene. It can be something you would like to put in your short story or novel, or simply an interesting scene that comes to mind. A romantic dinner between a young man and woman in a Paris café, for instance, or the final moments of a footy match. Write the same scene three times, in first, second and third person. For instance, first person: 'I remember the moment as if yesterday when I sat down beside Christine at this little café across the river from Notre Dame …'; second person, 'Christine, you were so radiant then, so full of life, that day you booked us in for lunch …'; third person: 'Christine and Matthew could hardly take their eyes off one another to look at the meagre but expensive croissants the waiter has just placed before them …' Your task: write a paragraph or two about the same scene from the three different grammatical voices. Take notice of the ways in which the change of voice changes the feel of what you have written.

13 Ursula Le Guin. *Steering the Craft: Exercises and Discussion on Story Writing for the Lone Navigator or the Mutinous Crew* (Portland: Eighth Mountain Press, 1998).

Chapter 14:

Show and Tell

> *'Don't tell me the moon is shining, show me the glint of light on broken glass.'*
>
> – Anton Chekhov[1]

Showing

In primary school the most popular activity of the week was Show-and-Tell. This is when students were asked, usually the day before, to bring in an object or to tell a story about themselves. The result was often a mixture of the two, that is, showing and telling. Telling everyone about your new puppy was okay, bringing in a photo to show was better, and having your parents bring in the puppy itself would make you the guaranteed star performer of the day.

Writing is much the same. We constantly hear that we should 'show' and not simply 'tell' the reader what is happening. The Russian novelist Anton Chekhov is reported to have once said: 'Don't tell me the moon is shining, show me the glint of light on broken glass.' This is great advice, but Chekhov didn't say it quite so succinctly. This well-known quote is a stylised summary of advice he gave to his brother about writing. In a letter from May 1886 he wrote: 'You'll have a moonlit night if you write that on the mill dam a piece of glass from a broken bottle glittered like a bright little star, and that the black shadow of a dog or a wolf rolled past like a ball."[2] While not so poetic as the version often attributed to him, the point is the same. Already in the late nineteenth century, budding writers were being advised to show and not simply to tell.

But what exactly does this mean? Many writers like to tell their readers what is happening. Sometimes this is because they do not trust the reader

1 Widely attributed to Anton Chekhov, who said something similar to this in advice to his brother. See below.

2 Avrahm Yarmolinsky, *The Unknown Chekhov. Stories and Other Writings Hitherto Untranslated by Anton Chekhov* (New York, Noonday Press, 1954), 14.

to 'get it right' unless they spell it out. Sometimes it is because they are in a hurry to progress their story to the next 'good bit', and telling is a lot easier and takes up fewer pages than showing. Sometimes it is because the main methods of showing – dialogue and descriptive writing – are difficult for the writer. Most often, it is a combination of these.

When I was writing my novel *Iscariot* I struggled regularly with this problem. I wanted the reader to know what Judas was thinking and feeling. I didn't want them to misunderstand a character who already had a two-thousand-year history of being misunderstood, or at least not being fully understood. I wanted the work, originally planned as a novella, to be kept succinct. So I kept telling the reader what Judas was thinking and feeling. But it was not effective writing.

For instance, I originally told the readers that, 'Judas went to the home of the high priest. He was desperate to give back the money. He had never thought matters would go so far. He wanted no part of this anymore. But the high priests had no time for him. Judas, who had been so important the night before, was now a nobody. They were not interested in the money. They were not interested in his conscience. They were not interested in Judas. They were too busy with their plot to get rid of Yeshua. Judas, near tears, threw the money to the floor and left.'

This paragraph gave a lot of important information. It helped me get to the bit where Judas goes to the courtyard of the palace to hear Pilate's judgement. But it is a key scene, and in my first attempt I rushed through it, telling the key information, but showing nothing. It is informative, but terrible storytelling. So I rewrote it as follows. Notice I no longer need to tell the reader that Judas was desperate, or that the priests were dismissive and had no time for him.

> Judas made his way through the courtyard and into the main house. There he found the high priests and the leaders of the Sanhedrin gathered in the largest of three inner courtyards. They were working through the night, preparing a case against the prisoner recently brought to the holding cell at the back of the complex.
>
> 'I need to speak with Caiaphas!' Judas demanded.
>
> The assembly gathered to look at the man who'd barged in, then turned back to their conversations.

Judas would not be ignored. 'I demand to speak to Caiaphas!' he shouted.

One of the priests standing nearby recognised Judas. 'You have your pay,' he said matter-of-factly. 'We have no more business with you.'

'I didn't accept money for *this*,' Judas pleaded. '*This* isn't what was supposed to happen. You said you only wanted to talk to the Teacher. I want no part in this.'

'Then leave,' said the priest curtly. 'Your role in this is done.'

Judas stood, holding his ground, refusing to move.

'Leave now,' said the priest, his voice becoming threatening, 'before you are thrown out.'

'You must take the money back,' Judas pleaded. 'I don't want it. I don't want any part in this.'

'We cannot take it back,' the priest declared. 'It's blood money. It was paid in exchange for a man's life. We cannot touch it.'

Judas stood silently. Blood money? Is that how they'd meant it? They had intended from the beginning to put Yeshua to death, and they'd paid him to betray him! How could he have been so blind? Judas took out the leather bag containing the thirty silver coins and flung them onto the floor. The coins clanged loudly against the polished floor stones of the courtyard. All became silent for a moment, turning their attention to Judas.

'The deal has been done,' said the priest to Judas, loud enough for all to hear. 'What you do with the money is your business. We will not touch it. You've betrayed your master and have received your payment. The deal has been done. Now leave us!'

Exasperated, defeated, lost, Judas turned to leave. Before he was even through the archway of the inner courtyard he heard the voices behind him rise once more to a hum of animated conversations. They were finished with him. Their attention was turned once again to the business at hand: how best to dispense with Yeshua.

I think you will agree that the second version is much better. We are allowed to watch the scene unfold and work out for ourselves what is going on. It is a good example of where telling needed to become showing.

Telling

But sometimes telling is necessary. It is not always wrong to tell a reader some bit of information. A story that relies entirely on dialogue and action description can become tedious. If there is no telling allowed, there is little role for a narrator. Sometimes the lengths we go to in order to show something are so awkward that the story no longer flows naturally. I have read manuscripts in which many pages were spent in meandering conversation with very little revealed until the pace of the story picked up again. In some cases these sections needed rewriting. In others, I advised the writer to just give us a summary paragraph of what happened so we could move more quickly from the preceding scene to the one that followed. To take another example from *Iscariot*, I originally went through much effort to get Yeshua, Judas and the rest of the disciples back to Galilee. I wanted to show how Galilee differed from Judea. I wanted to highlight that Judas was the only non-Galilean among the twelve and that all of this was new to him. I had quite a few exchanges of dialogue between Judas and John. I threw in a few comments from the others. I described different scenes as they came upon them. The whole thing was becoming a long and tedious travelogue. I had plenty of things to show that were coming up in the story, I just needed to get them to Galilee with a reminder that Judas was the odd one out, the only non-Galilean in the group. In the end, I abandoned the three pages I had written, with all of my attempts at showing, and simply gave the following paragraph of telling.

> As Yeshua and the Twelve neared the Sea of Galilee, their pace quickened. For Judas, this was new territory. For the others, it was home. As they passed through the hills south of the Sea of Galilee, Judas was struck by the greenness of the countryside in comparison with the region around Jerusalem. The pastures were covered in thick grass, and the steep hillsides and ravines were filled with trees spreading their canopy far above the ground. As the group crested a range of hills, the massive Sea of Galilee came into view before

> them. Judas moved to the front of the group to take in the sweeping vista of its blue waters shimmering in the late afternoon sun. How different it was to the pale white of the Great Salt Sea that lay just a few miles east of Jerusalem. And this sea, Judas was assured by his companions, teemed with life, providing enough fish to feed the entire region. Beyond the sea he could see the great snow-capped mountain called Hermon towering in the distance. On the other side of it lay the famed city of Damascus.

One of the greatest writers of the nineteenth century, Leo Tolstoy, began his novel *Anna Karenina* with a famous opening sentence, then followed it up with two paragraphs of pure 'telling' that allowed him to bring readers up to speed before he went back to 'showing' us what was happening.

> Happy families are all alike; every unhappy family is unhappy in its own way.
>
> Everything at the Oblonsky's was topsy-turvy. Oblonsky's wife had found out that he had been having an affair with the French governess who used to live with them, and told him she could no longer stay under the same roof with him. This was the third day things had been this way, and not only the married couple themselves, but the family and the whole household were painfully aware of it. Everyone in the house felt that there was no sense in living together, and that people who had casually dropped into any inn would have more connection with each other than they, the Oblonsky family and household.
>
> Oblonsky's wife refused to leave her room; he himself hadn't been home for three days. The children were running around the house as though lost; the English governess had had a quarrel with the housekeeper and written to a friend of hers asking her to look out for a new job for her; the day before the cook had picked dinnertime to go out; the kitchen maid and the coachman had given notice.[3]

Perhaps the best advice is not 'show, don't tell,' but rather 'show *and* tell.' The trick is knowing when, and how, to do each.

---

3 Leo Tolstoy. *Anna Karenina.* (New Haven: Yale University Press, 2015), 1.

Showing and telling the truth

In his book, *The Lie That Tells a Truth*, John Dufresne argued that fiction is essentially stuff that is made up, or lies. But that doesn't mean that it cannot and should not also be the truth. 'Fiction,' clarified Dufresne, 'is telling the truth, not telling the facts.'[4]

It is the writer's job to tell the truth, to show readers what the world was, is or can be. We must tell the truth, even if we have to make stuff up to do it. That is what good fiction is: lies that tell the truth.

But truth-telling can be more difficult than it might seem. Mary Anne Evans, aka George Eliot, saw this clearly.

> So I am content to tell my simple story, without trying to make things seem better than they were; dreading nothing, indeed, but falsity, which, in spite of one's best efforts, there is reason to dread. Falsehood is so easy, truth so difficult. The pencil is conscious of a delightful facility in drawing a griffin – the longer the claws, and the larger the wings, the better; but that marvellous facility which we mistook for genius is apt to forsake us when we want to draw a real unexaggerated lion. Examine your words well, and you will find that even when you have no motive to be false, it is a very hard thing to say the exact truth, even about your own immediate feelings – much harder than to say something fine about them which is not the exact truth.[5]

Tell the truth. Write fiction if you must. But never lie to your readers. Never show them something that is false, fake, or a deception.

As a reader, I want to know the truth. I do not like being lied to. I can live with an author disagreeing with me, with having a radically different worldview to my own, but not with being lied to, that is, having a world-view portrayed that the author knows not to be true. As a reader, I do not want to be told about a young girl who sees her entire family tragically killed, then finds a new home and lives happily ever after. I know the world is not like that. Do not show me a man who is corrupted by the pursuit or power and wealth who then one day sees the light and walks away unscathed. I will not believe you. Do not show me characters

---

4 John Dufresne. *The Lie That Tells a Truth. A Guide to Writing Fiction* (New York: W.W. Norton, 2003), 15.

5 George Eliot, *Adam Bede*, (Edinburgh: John Blackwood, 1859), ch 17.

behaving selfishly and hurting others to get what they want, then try to convince me that they are really good. I won't buy it.

If you are a Christian writer, don't tell me that God is good and gracious and forgiving if you do not believe it yourself. I will see through it. Themes of brokenness and reconciliation, sin and salvation need to be explored with the conviction of their truth, irrespective of the fictional characters and events employed to tell these truths.

I may not always like hearing it, but tell me the truth. Tell me the truth as honestly as you can – even if you have to invent and populate an entire fictitious world to do it.

Chapter 15:

Writing Dialogue

> *'There's a paradox about dialogue in fiction, which is that in order to achieve the effortless-looking illusion of real speech, the writer has to apply a lot of effort.'*
>
> – Kate Grenville[1]

Tim and Sandra entered the classroom late. They were always late.

'Glad you could join us,' I said, with more than a hint of irritation. They didn't appear to notice.

'Wonder what made you two late,' giggled Denise.

Sandra simply gave her a knowing smile, then sat down next to Tim. Sandra and Tim love my class, or so they tell me. That's where they met at the beginning of the term. I've nothing against love, but I wish they'd met in someone else's class.

'So, what's on the menu today?' Michael asked, eager to get started, now that everyone was present. I'm not sure how much Michael actually enjoys creative writing, but he does seem obsessed with getting his money's worth. I think he'd complain if I ever let class out early. But that's not likely to happen. I've never been that organised.

'Dialogue,' I announced calmly, looking around the table at the faces of the dozen students for a reaction. I got none.

Dialogue is one of the most difficult skills for many writers to master. We have conversations every day, but writing them down in a correct and interesting way, and in a manner that progresses our story, often proves difficult. There is no magic fix for writing good dialogue apart from plenty of practice. But keeping the following points in mind is helpful.

The purpose of dialogue. We include dialogue in our stories because real characters speak. If our dialogue is too sparse, we are reduced to

---

1 Kate Grenville, *The Writing Book. A Workbook for Fiction Writers*. (Sydney: Allen & Unwin, 1990), 101.

long, uninteresting paragraphs which tell the reader what we think they need to know. Dialogue, on the other hand, is one of the best ways of showing the reader what is happening or what a character is like. There is no need to describe how rude a certain character is and how much the other characters dislike him, when you can show this by what your character says, how and when he says it, and how others react to him.

The correct format of dialogue. Your dialogue will look better on the page and be easier to follow if you observe certain standard conventions of dialogue writing. The most important and obvious 'rule' – and also the one most people tend to forget – is that each new speaker requires a new paragraph. It doesn't matter if they only say one word, or if they simply think their response or nod in agreement. Perhaps you introduce your character's comment with the narrator's voice. For instance:

Clearly taken aback, Sarah composed herself before simply stating: 'I had expected more of you.'

In this example, the new paragraph would not begin with Sarah's actual words, but with the narrator's introduction of them. A good way to discover how to use dialogue is to look through one of the novels you have recently read and see how the author sets it out.

The other 'rule' that is generally followed is that dialogue should be set off using quotation marks. Whether you chose to use single or double quotation marks is a matter of personal taste, but the trend is strongly in favour of single quotation marks. Using quotations marks is important to help distinguish dialogue from the narrator's comments introducing the dialogue, and other such bits of information interspersed within the conversation. Occasionally an author will use italics for dialogue, but this mostly occurs to indicate something unusual about the speech, for instance that it is only what a person is thinking, or it is in a foreign language, or the conversation partners are communicating telepathically – or via social media.

Narrator's voice within dialogue. The role of the narrator within dialogue is to introduce speakers, point out things about the tone of voice that the reader may not pick up, and give us any other necessary information about the physical gestures of those speaking and their surroundings. Without this function, the dialogue will read like a mere transcript of a recorded conversation; flat, lifeless, and lacking the necessary information to understand the entire context of what is taking place.

Speech attribution. One function of the narrator is the task of attributing speech to the right characters. While writers often wish to avoid the annoying repetition of 'he said' and 'she said', overuse of phrases such as, 'he said with more than a hint of expectant passion in his voice' can become a distraction. If it is clear from the context who is saying what, there may be dialogue exchanges in which nothing apart from the dialogue itself need be recorded. If 'he said' and 'she said' need breaking up, stick with simple alternatives and make longer comments sparingly.

Kate Grenville describes some of the diverse ways the writer may attribute speech without simply repeating 'he said' and 'she said.'

> Attributes are a necessary evil. Too many give a bit of dialogue a monotonous limping feeling. Too few and you lose track of who's saying what. It's tempting to break the monotony with the help of a thesaurus, which has any number of substitutes for 'he said': he can expostulate, moan, whisper, shout, interject and so on, but unless you're writing comedy the thesaurus is not the answer . . . . A much more graceful solution is [when] . . . the pieces of dialogue are separated from each other by small actions or thoughts. These give the reader the clue as to who is speaking. This has the other advantage of providing some of the non-verbal dimension of a conversation: gestures, body language, tone of voice, those pauses between comments. Sometimes characters have such very different ways of speaking that attribution can be pared right down to the minimum. Each piece of dialogue can contain some tiny piece of information that tells us which character is speaking.[2]

Use of slang and accents. Mastering slang and accents is not easy. If you are unable to write dialogue for a heavily accented Irish woman, then cast someone easier to write in this role. The important thing, apart from not taking on a task beyond your current abilities, is to make sure your dialogue matches the speaker. A school child is going to speak differently than a teacher, and an astrophysicist differently

2 Kate Grenville. *The Writing Book*, 103f.

than a sporting hero. Practise listening to real people. Write down their dialogue, giving attention to the speech patterns, slang and non-verbal aspects of communication.

In the following example of dialogue from *Of Mice and Men*, John Steinbeck captures something of the essence of the speech of rural American farm workers in the 1930s.

> 'These guys jus' come,' said Slim by way of introduction.
>
> 'Glad ta meet ya,' the big man said. 'My name's Carlson.'
>
> 'I'm George Milton. This here's Lennie Small.'
>
> 'Glad to meet ya,' Carlson said again. 'He ain't very small.' He chuckled softly at his joke. 'Ain't small at all,' he repeated. 'Meant to ask you, Slim – how's your bitch? I seen she wasn't under your wagon this morning.'
>
> 'She slang her pups last night,' said Slim. 'Nine of 'em. I drowned four of 'em right off. She couldn't feed that many.'
>
> 'Got five left, huh?'
>
> 'Yeah, five. I kept the biggest.'
>
> 'What kinda dogs you think they're gonna be?'
>
> 'I dunno,' said Slim. 'Some kinda shepherds, I guess.'[3]

But be careful not to overdo slang, accents and dialect. It can become difficult to read, and in some cases, can appear that you are making fun of those who speak with a particular accent or come from another socio-economic group. While the conversation in the example of Steinbeck is easy to read, such dialogue can only be written well if the writer has spent much time listening to the way real people speak. As Stephen King wrote: 'Dialogue is a skill best learned by people who enjoy talking and listening to others – particularly listening, picking up accents, rhythms, dialect and slang of various groups.'[4]

---

3 John Steinbeck. *Of Mice and Men* [1937] (New York: Bantam Books, 1963), 39.

4 Stephen King. *On Writing. A Memoir of the Craft.* (London: Hodder & Stoughton, 2012), 214.

Exercise: Eavesdropping

One of the best ways to master writing realistic dialogue is to practice recording real conversations. During the next week try to listen in to some real conversations: on the bus, at a restaurant, in the doctor's waiting room, etc. When you get back to your pen and notepad, do not attempt to reproduce a verbatim of every word spoken, but try to convey a sense of the conversation. Make sure that you relay something of the setting and the non-verbals. If the conversation is taking place in a fast food restaurant or if one of the conversationalists is sad, angry, etc., the reader should be able to pick this up from your narrator's comments interspersed through the dialogue.

CHAPTER 16:

'In the Beginning'

'A story has no beginning and no end, only points of entry.'

– Carlos Ruiz Zafón[1]

From a structural standpoint, most works of longer fiction can be divided into beginnings, middle sections and endings. Each of these sections merit special, individual attention. We will start in the obvious place – the beginning.

Beginnings

It has become something of a cliché among writers that the worst ever opening sentence for a novel is: 'It was a dark and stormy night.' The line has been satirised and even spawned a competition to see who can add to the sentence to produce the worst opening paragraph. While the line first appeared in Washington Irving's satirical *A History of New York* (1809) it was its use as the opening sentence of Edward Bulwer-Lytton's otherwise forgettable 1830 novel *Paul Clifford* that brought it infamy.[2] It has become such a cliché of bad writing that good writers sometimes deliberately employ it as something of an insiders' joke. Madeleine L'Engle, for instance, used the line as the opening sentence for *A Wrinkle in Time* and appears to have done so as a homage to Charles Schulz's character Snoopy, who begins most of his stories with this much-maligned sentence.

Despite all this exposure, one still comes across inexperienced writers who open their stories with something along these same lines. Some years back I was given the manuscript of a novel to read which began, 'It was a stormy and dark winter night.' The author was not using the sentence satirically, or for a laugh, or to pay homage to Snoopy, but

1 Carlos Ruiz Zafón, *The Labyrinth of the Spirits*, tr. Lucia Graves (Melbourne: Text Publishing, 2017), 789.

2 By the way, Bulwer-Lytton also gave us the phrases 'the pen is mightier than the sword,' 'the great unwashed' and 'the almighty dollar.'

simply thought it was a very good way to begin his novel. But just why is this such a bad way to open a novel – or for that matter – a short story? Apart from sounding clichéd and overusing adjectives, the sentence really doesn't say anything. It doesn't prick our curiosity, introduce a character or open up a mystery. In fact, saying the night was 'dark' is obvious. And Bulwer-Lytton didn't help his case by continuing on from this line with the words; 'the rain fell in torrents – except at occasional intervals.' In other words, he told us not only that the night was dark, but that it was raining hard, which is what generally happens in storms, except of course, as he pointed out, when it wasn't raining hard!

One of the more famous opening sentences in recent literature is Tolkien's, 'In a hole in the ground there lived a hobbit,' a sentence he says came to him as if a revelation while marking exam papers. In this simple sentence he has already introduced, or at least indicated, the main character, and has certainly pricked the reader's curiosity. What is a hobbit? And what is it doing in a hole in the ground? The very next sentences go on to answer some of these questions.

A good opening, and not only the first sentence, is the writer's best and often only chance to hook the reader. If the opening sentences and paragraphs do not engage the reader, they are unlikely to read further. A good beginning generally seeks to do two main things: introduce the main character or characters, and introduce some point of tension – a question to be answered, a mystery to be solved or a quest to be fulfilled.

This is the writer's contract with the reader. The writer is committing to deliver on promises made in the opening. Along the way little hints may be dropped, but the final resolution of the plot will be reserved for the end of the story. This is why the reader keeps reading. John Marsden, author of the *Tomorrow when the War Began* series, put it well: 'All good openings raise more questions than they answer.'[3]

I have often heard it said that editors at publishing houses will make a decision about whether or not a manuscript has merit after the first twenty pages. After having worked for some time as an editor for a publisher, I can say that this is not true. I would never waste my time reading twenty pages of a badly written or boring manuscript. If you

3 John Marsden. *Everything I Know about Writing*, 73.

cannot impress me and pique my curiosity within the first three pages (at the most), I am unlikely to read any further, unless you are a close friend or relative and I feel obliged to explain to you in some detail precisely why we will not be publishing your novel. The potential customer in a book store will certainly read no further than this, so why should a publisher, who would be taking a financial risk on these same customers buying your book? If you have a good hook to your story, a great scene, a wonderful description, an intriguing character, use it and use it quickly. I once had a writer ask why we rejected his manuscript. I explained that there was nothing in the first chapter that gave any real indication of the plot, aroused my curiosity, suggested some mystery that needed to be solved or endeared the main character to me in any way.

'Oh,' he said, 'that stuff doesn't really begin to happen until chapter three. The first two chapters simply give the background context.'

'Well,' I suggested, 'perhaps you should consider beginning your novel with chapter three.'

It's a radical thought, but sometimes a writer needs to let go of a cherished opening that just doesn't work or is not necessary. Many successful novels actually begin with what was originally the second or third chapter, and are much better for it.

The point is, before sending your novel out into the wide and scary world of publishing, make sure you go over the first few pages very carefully, asking yourself whether you have done all that you can to make a potential reader want to keep reading. You must start on a high note, as no reader apart from close friends and family (and not even all of these) is going to read on, waiting for the story to get interesting.

Writers often speak of making a 'pitch' to a publisher. Opportunities to do this are even arranged at many writing events where authors have anywhere from five to ten minutes to convince a publisher to consider their manuscript more fully. The reality is that your opening paragraphs are the best and often only pitch you will be able to make for your novel. Don't hold back. If you cannot sell the story here, you might need to consider the possibility that there is nothing to sell, or that you are beginning the story in the wrong place, or in the wrong way.

CHAPTER 17:

The Middle Game

> *'Good literature has little or nothing to do with trivial fancies such as "inspiration" or "having something to tell" and more with the engineering of language, with the architecture of narrative, with the painting of textures, with the timbres and colours of the staging, with the cinematography of words, and the music that can be produced by an orchestra of ideas.'*
>
> – Carlos Ruiz Zafón[1]

Students of chess divide the game into three phases: the opening, the middle game, and the end game. Every good chess player knows that without a good opening, the game is lost, and lost early. Playing the final stages and achieving (or avoiding) checkmate is equally important. Most chess players spend much of their time studying and practising openings and endgames. But the middle game is often neglected, to the detriment of the player. The middle game is the long, less exciting part of the game where the player builds on their opening and works toward their endgame. It is easy to overlook, but this is where most of the hard work takes place.

Writing a novel is much the same. Openings and endings are exciting to talk about, and we give much attention to these. But most of the hard work gets done in those long stretches of narrative and dialogue in between. In a novel, the middle section is by far the most lengthy and often the most vital. Yet the principles involved in its construction are often overlooked in favour of time devoted to learning how to write beginnings and endings.

If the writer establishes a contract with the reader in the opening of a story or novel, then it is in the middle that reminders and tantalising hints should be given of what this resolution might be as all the pieces are brought into play that will be necessary for a satisfying conclusion. The middle of a novel is not the place to add filler that plays no role in

1 Carlos Ruiz Zafón, *The Labyrinth of the Spirits*, 764f.

the final resolution. In a good novel there will be no leftover pieces when the puzzle is put together. If you keep this in mind, you're less likely to veer off course.

The middle of a novel is often the most difficult part. This is the place where many authors get 'writer's block.' While we may come up with a really gripping opening and have a good conclusion to our story in mind, all the work of filling in details about characters and events in order to finally get to our envisioned dénouement can be hard work.

I have had an idea for a particular novel in my head since university days. I began the novel several times, then became stuck. I knew how I wanted the story to end, so several years ago I wrote the final chapters. This gave me renewed energy to go back and finish the beginning. I have rewritten those first and final chapters several times over the last three decades. But there is much work to be done in the middle – perhaps too much. The novel inevitably got put to one side time and again as I pursued other 'easier' projects. Thirty years after I first conceived the idea, I still think the manuscript has one of the best openings and endings I've written. But without a substantive middle, they are entirely pointless. The hard work on this particular manuscript remains to be done. There are no shortcuts. The harsh reality is that writing the bits of the novel between the beginning and the ending is often a struggle, especially if you set yourself a big task in the opening, with the promise of unravelling a series of interconnected plots or mysteries.

The occasional side plot, so long as it contributes to the overall storyline, can help to fill the pages. But the bottom line is that the middle of a novel is the place where an author shows that he or she can sustain interest in the story and characters and bring the narrative to the place where the conclusion actually works. However slowly the pace of your narrative moves in the middle section of your novel, it must still always be progressing toward the conclusion. Readers can tolerate a slow pace, especially if the writing is good. But they will not tolerate a storyline that diverts into endless side stories that ultimately do not move the main plotline forward. There are few better ways to lose the interest and goodwill of your readers than by filling the middle of your novel with material that simply does not progress the story.

Also, your readers cannot see the forests, city streets, rooms, etc. in which your action takes place. In the middle sections of your novel you must not only narrate the action and dialogue of your characters, but also describe the important settings where the action or dialogue takes place. As with everything else, there are less and more interesting ways to do this. I could say, for instance, that I am currently writing these lines while staying at an old homestead consisting of a cottage, a large shed, an old milk house, assorted small sheds and some old equipment left lying about. But that's not very interesting. Why not instead say something like: 'The centuries old cottage, now restored as a weekender, is the only building, apart from the corrugated iron shed adjacent to it, still in use. The two-stall dairy and granary have long ago been abandoned. There are few reminders – a lone milk can, a couple of rusting tools, and an old tractor tyre – that for more than a hundred years this had been a working farm on which people struggled to make a living and raise their children. A 1938 Chevrolet truck sits under an elm tree with a seed spreader still optimistically attached to its decaying, wooden bed, ready for a planting that never came. In the front yard an aged willow, now dying, still contains the remnants of what had once been a tree house.'

Can you see the difference? I described the same old homestead. But the bare description of the place does little to enliven the imagination. A closer look around the homestead, however, reveals a story of generations of ultimately futile effort to make a go of farming in a low rainfall area. The setting and people in the middle of your stories and novels should be brought to life with such descriptions – but be careful not to overdo it. Describe in detail what needs description. But don't spend so much time portraying the settings that your reader forgets what the story is about that you are telling.

You can also put a bit of suspense into your descriptions which will help carry the story along rather than simply painting a visual image of the setting. Susanna Clarke, in her delightful *Jonathan Strange and Mr Norrell*, describes the home and library of the mysterious Mr. Norrell. She does it in such a way that she communicates to the reader that there is something very unusual about this house – a mystery that will need resolving.

> Mr Norrell led the other two gentlemen along a passage – a very ordinary passage, thought Mr Segundus, paneled and floored with well-polished oak, and smelling of beeswax; then there was a staircase, or perhaps only three or four steps; and then another passage where the air was somewhat colder and the floor of good York stone: all entirely unremarkable. (Unless the second passage has come before the staircase or steps? Or had there in truth been a staircase at all?) Mr Secundus was one of those happy gentlemen who can always say whether they face north or south, east or west . . . – but in Mr Norrell's house his gift deserted him. . . .
>
> The library was perhaps a little smaller than the drawing-room they had just quitted. There was a noble fire in the hearth and all was comfort and quiet. Yet . . . the light within the room did not seem to accord with the three tall twelve-paned windows, so that once again Mr Segundus was made uncomfortable by a persistent feeling that there ought to have been other candles in the room, other windows or another fire to account for the light. What windows there were looked out upon a wide expanse of dusky English rain so that Mr Segundus could not make out the view nor guess where in the house they stood.[2]

In this example, even something as basic as a chunk of descriptive writing is doing its job of advancing the plot, moving the narrative ever closer to its conclusion.

Don't rush through the middle section, hurrying to get to your ending. If you savour the experience, and work your way steadily forward, the reader will also not feel rushed. They will instead feel that the middle of your novel is not endless pages to be gotten through, but an integral part of the story to be enjoyed.

Exercise: Writing descriptively

Take an ordinary room; the one, perhaps, where you do most of your writing, and bring it to life with a vivid description that helps the reader feel like they know this room – as if they are there with you.

---

2 Susanna Clarke. *Jonathan Strange and Mr Norrell* (London: Bloomsbury, 2004), 12f.

Chapter 18:

A Good Ending is Hard to Find

> *'Good endings make sense, evoke emotion like contentment, anger, sadness, or curiosity, shift the reader's perspective, or open her mind to new ideas. They do not confuse or cast the whole story as a hoax. Good endings bring the hero, and more importantly, the reader to some kind of destination – even if it's a trap.'*
>
> – Alex Coyne[1]

The first time I ran the 1600 metres at the Bay-Sheffield, a famous running carnival held just after Christmas every year on the Adelaide foreshore community of Glenelg, I found myself unexpectedly leading the race for the last two laps – well, for almost all of the last two laps. Coming down the home straight, with a couple thousand punters yelling and screaming around the outer edges of the grass track, I felt overwhelmed by the interest and enthusiasm for a foot race. I had never before experienced anything like it. The months of training, weekly track work, Sunday afternoon long runs, were paying off. My strategy to make a strong move early and 'go for it' had worked. Now here I was, running to the tape that was only 50 metres, 40 metres, 30 metres, 20 metres, 10 metres away. I lifted my arms in celebration and tried not to look too strained as I broke the tape. That is when the two runners who had been making a desperate late charge from behind edged past me to claim first and second places by less than 30 centimetres.

Afterward our club coach said: 'Great race, Mark, apart for the last ten metres.' The entire race was over in just under 4 minutes and 30 seconds. And I had run well and according to plan for all but the last two of those seconds. What happened? Easy. I had done the work. I was exhausted. I felt the race was over. I could coast the last ten metres across the line, like Usain Bolt in the Olympic 100 metres at Beijing! But I wasn't Usain Bolt – and the race wasn't over.

---

1 Alex Coyne, 'Making Ends Meet: How to Write a Good Ending to a Story,' in *RE:Fiction. The Fiction Writers Magazine.* https://Refection.com/articles/making-ends-meet. Accessed 23.1.2019.

You may think that it was a silly and careless thing to do. It was. The reality is that many writers do the very same thing with their novels. They spend years researching, doing character sketches, revising and editing. By the time they are at the end of their story they can see the finish line. They are eager to send off their manuscript to a publisher, become famous, and move on to their next project. But in all too many cases they take their eye off the finish line and coast across, thinking that so much good work has already been done that they can take it easy. They just want the novel to be finished and see it in print.

But a second-rate ending can spoil an otherwise first-rate novel. In a footrace, no one remembers in what position you were running during the race, only in what position you finished. Likewise, readers remember how the novel ended, and what feeling it left them with. They have spent perhaps $20 or $30 dollars on your book, and have invested a few evenings or weekends of their time in reading it. They do not want to be left feeling that the author has coasted through to the finish, his or her mind already on other things.

It is all too easy for authors to fall short of expectations with their endings. After all, most authors have far more experience writing beginnings than they do endings. How many novels, for instance, have you started, but never finished? And if you have completed a novel, how many times have you reworked the opening chapter, as it was often the very first thing you wrote? And how often has the ending been written only a few days or weeks before you sent your off manuscript, never giving yourself the opportunity to review it with the same thoroughness and care you gave to your opening?

If you cannot hook your reader in the first two to four pages, they are not likely to continue reading your novel. Every successful writer knows this. But what few writers are told is that if the last two to four pages do not shine and leave an impression, the reader will not likely read your next novel – or recommend the one they have just finished to a friend. Last impressions are also important.

So what should a novel achieve in its ending? This, of course, depends somewhat on the type of novel you are writing. In a romance, the reader wants the protagonist to find true love; in a crime story, they expect the crime to be solved; in the first volume of a trilogy, they expect some significant resolution, but also enough lingering questions to lure them back for books two and three. But there are some things that are true of a good conclusion for any novel.

Twelve marks of a good ending

1. A good conclusion ties up or resolves all the loose ends. If it does not, the reader is frustrated either because they are left wondering what happened to some of the main characters, or they feel they have been made to read a number of side stories that in the end turned out to play no role in the overall narrative or its resolution.
2. A good conclusion really does bring the story to an end. A cliff-hanger is not a conclusion – even for book one of your planned trilogy.
3. Your main protagonist or protagonists must be central in your conclusion (even if they are not physically present). Readers have stuck with your story this far because they care about your main character and they want to know what happens to him or her.
4. A good conclusion doesn't dump information in the final pages or paragraphs. If you have a lot of plot-lines to bring together and tie up, begin doing this early, maybe even a couple of chapters out from the end, rather than giving your readers a list of everything that happens to each main character in the last couple of paragraphs.
5. A good conclusion maintains the pace, tone and quality of writing that has preceded it. Don't let your writing and editing standards slip at the end.
6. A good conclusion doesn't cheat. Readers do not like to be wondering how in the world a situation might be resolved, or how everything that has occurred in the story thus far is possible, only to read on the last line: 'Jenny realised that the sound she heard was not sirens, but her own alarm clock going off. It had all been a dream.' This is not a clever way to end a story, though many inexperienced writers seem to believe otherwise.
7. A good conclusion may be unexpected, but it must be plausible in the context of the narrative. In old plays, an intervention or ending was often contrived by lowering an angel or a god (the *deus ex machina*!)

down onto the stage with a skyhook to intervene and sort things out. A narrative that is so complex that only an alien incursion can resolve your plot twists is either a very poor plotline, or deserves a much more sophisticated ending than the one you have given it.

8. Surprise endings work with some novels, but only if there have been hints scattered throughout the novel. If no one saw the ending coming because it was completely random, they will not be satisfied or impressed. If, however, as soon as they read the ending they are left thinking: 'Why didn't I see that coming? It is all makes sense now' then you will have satisfied readers. The movie 'The Sixth Sense' had a surprise ending. It worked very well because as soon as the viewer saw it, they realised they had not been misled. There had been plenty of clues along the way, they had simply been allowed to see what they wanted to see.
9. Good endings come in ones. Do not have layers of endings, as if you could not decide which one to go with, or simply could not bear to finish your novel. Watch the last twenty-five minutes of the movie 'AI' sometime. The story comes to a perfectly good and satisfying conclusion, then inexplicably continues on to add another conclusion. And while the audience is left pondering why the movie is still going on, a third, and even more implausible conclusion is added. By the time the credits finally rolled in the screening I attended, many in the audience were left cursing Spielberg for wasting their time. That is not how you want readers to walk away from your novel!
10. A good ending is a beautiful ending. There have been many brilliant victories in the history of chess. Perhaps the most famous was the game still known as 'The Immortal Game'. It was played during a break in a scheduled tournament in a London café on 21 June 1851 by Lionel Kieseritzky and reigning world champion Adolf Andersen. There was no prize money, and no title was at stake. The game is remembered entirely for the beauty and brilliance of the last eight moves! In other words, it is not just getting to your destination that matters, it is how you get there.
11. A good chess player masters king and pawn endings. Pawns are often viewed by young chess players as the most uninteresting pieces, and

often overlooked, because their moves are so limited. A good writer masters the ability to make subtle moves and use small details and techniques to inch their protagonist toward a conclusion that few may have seen coming, but which, in retrospect, was inevitable.

12. A good ending should not be formulaic. Some writing experts will suggest a formula to follow, and some book series even require this. In these cases the required ending for a certain kind of story will have certain key features. The publishers assume that this is what the readers want. And perhaps many of them do. But such endings are not great endings. There might be some boxes that need to be ticked in your ending, given the expectations of your particular genre, but try to include at least something that is not what the reader was expecting. If your ending is too predictable and formulaic, readers may struggle with the motivation to finish your novel when they already know all the important points of what will and must happen at the end.

Tips for improving your endgame

1. Read the conclusions of well-written novels and make a note of the things they do and don't do.
2. Think of a decent novel you have read in which the conclusion didn't quite satisfy you. Write an alternate ending.
3. If the previous exercise seems too difficult, think of a novel you have read recently with an ending that really left you wanting to read more from that author. Rewrite it in such a way so as to completely destroy it, but as subtly as you can. Note well how you ruined a perfectly good ending. Do not do the same with your novel.
4. Write your conclusion early in your novel writing process. You might even try writing the concluding paragraphs first! If you know where you are going, you might find it easier to get there, and have everything make more sense once you do arrive. It also gives you more time to revise and refine your ending.
5. "Just finish the novel!" – the exasperated words of many partners and friends of writers.

Exercise: Alternate endings

If you are currently working on a novel or shorter story, you likely have an ending already in mind. When writers get a certain ending in their head it's hard for them to see any other alternatives. For this exercise, think of a very different way that your story might end and sketch out an alternative ending (no more than two or three paragraphs). Does the new ending have any advantages over the one you already had in mind? In what ways does it change the feel of the story? You may surprise yourself. You may even choose to go with the alternative ending for your story. Good writers never close themselves off to alternative possibilities.

CHAPTER 19:

Creative Non-Fiction

> *'Creative nonfiction is like jazz – it's a rich mix of flavors, ideas, and techniques, some of which are newly invented and others as old as writing itself.'*
>
> – Lee Gutkind[1]

Creative non-fiction is a relatively new concept. Traditionally, prose writing was spoken of as either fiction or non-fiction. You really couldn't have it both ways. Then teachers of creative writing began to realise that just because someone is writing non-fiction it doesn't mean they cannot use creative elements, or that the book has to be dead boring. So writing classes and books began to appear under the title of 'creative non-fiction.'

As an academic, I have written a number of non-fiction books. I would like to think they were all creative and interesting, but most were not. Many were meant to be of interest only to other experts in the field. I gave complimentary copies, of course, to my parents, but with the warning that they should never attempt to actually read them! No one would suggest that these were works of creative non-fiction.

But I have also written non-fiction books which are easier to read, more interesting for general readers, and involved much more creativity on my part as an author. I would not hesitate to label these efforts as creative non-fiction. So what is the difference? Quite simply, when non-fiction works employ the kind of creativity and techniques that make them not only informative, but also entertaining (e.g., show don't tell, dialogue, etc.), it is reasonable to speak about them as creative non-fiction.[1]

1 Lee Gutkind, 'What is Creative Nonfiction?' in *Creative Nonfiction* (Issue #0). www.creativenonfiction.org/online-reading/what-creative-nonfiction. See also Gutkind, *You Can't Make This Stuff Up: The Complete Guide to Writing Creative Nonfiction – from Memoir to Literary Journalism and Everything in Between.* (Boston: Da Capo Press, 2012).

Creative non-fiction and biography

One of the most common types of non-fiction writing is biography. As it is also a non-fiction genre with which I have some experience, I will use this genre to illustrate how non-fiction writing can also be creative writing. The basic principles, of course, can be applied to other genres, ranging from travel and cooking, to self-help and history.

Biographies are by definition non-fiction. If you create an intentionally and overtly fictionalised version of a real person's life, that is historical fiction (or perhaps political biography!), but not biography. Because a person's life story is largely fixed by the things they actually did and said, it might appear difficult to understand where elements of creativity can enter in. But biography writers make many decisions about how to tell the story that can and should employ strong elements of creativity. The writer of biography is not obliged to begin their story with the subject's birth, and finish with their death or the present state of their life. The first major biography I wrote was *Graham Clark. The Man Who Invented the Bionic Ear* (Allen & Unwin, 2015). While aspects of Graham's childhood were important, it seemed a rather pedestrian place to begin the story. So I chose to begin with the day of the first successful bionic ear operation. In some ways it was really the end of the story, and some warned me that by revealing the end in the first chapter people might not want to keep reading. But given that Graham's success was well-known, and the sub-title was to be, 'The Man Who Invented the Bionic Ear,' there seemed little possibility for suspense in saving this revelation for the end. So I chose to begin at the height of the action, then go back and show how Graham arrived at this milestone in the history of medicine.

I also had to decide how to portray Graham and how to portray the opposition he encountered as he went about his life's work. I had to decide what details and stories of Graham's life were interesting and fit within the larger narrative, and which did not. I deliberately included a bit of humour, but had to be careful to keep it subtle so that the overriding story was a serious one. I opted for short, self-contained chapters that would suit the modern, busy reader. This meant each chapter had to reach some kind of provisional resolution, but also hint at another problem to be overcome, so that the reader would want to continue on to the following chapter.

Graham was also a committed Christian and had been since his student days. His faith played an important role in his life as a scientist and both he and I were keen that this should come through in the biography. But how was this to be done without it looking like these elements were awkwardly inserted into the story, or portraying them in such a way that the book was no longer suitable for the mainstream market at which it was aimed? A mixture of small bits of information mixed into the story, sometimes with a bit of humour, and a couple of chapters that dealt openly with Graham's faith, worked best.

In the end, I drew as much upon my skills in creative writing as I did upon those of an historical researcher. It was the process of writing Graham's life story that drove home to me that creative non-fiction is a distinct and important category of writing.

I carried over the lessons learned in writing the biography of Graham Clark to my next biography, a life of Martin Luther written for the 500th anniversary of the Reformation. The book, *Martin Luther: A Wild Boar in the Lord's Vineyard* (Morning Star, 2107) was more academic in character than the Graham Clark biography. So many books had been written about Luther's life over the years that it was a challenge to find creative ways to make my re-telling of the story interesting. But Luther's life was a remarkable one, with a host of minor characters and events that one could never make up, and I was a storyteller. My job was to tell the story well and creatively and not turn an exciting and eventful life into the dry bones of a pedantically remembered history, or another bit of Protestant hagiography.

I decided to begin the story of Luther's life with the day of his posting of the ninety-five theses, then go back and show how he got to that point and what happened afterward. I decided also to go with short chapters, as I had with the Graham Clark biography, with their own mini-introductions and conclusions, as well as hooks to make the reader want to continue on to the next chapter. I discovered that there was room for a great deal of creativity in the telling of the story, while remaining faithful to the known historical facts. The book was an academic work, to be sure, but also a creative work. It was little things that made the difference, like describing some of the scenes, introducing interesting secondary characters, adding some suspense to the narration of individual episodes, and exploring the very human side of the Reformer.

There are times in which the application of the techniques of creative non-fiction can be quite overt. The most difficult book I have ever written was the story of my son's mental illness and suicide. After his death, I found there was nothing to give his younger brother and sister to read that would help them talk about what had happened. People just don't write middle-grade and Young Adult stories about suicide. Yet in Australia alone approximately three thousand deaths by suicide occur each year, and many of these directly impact children and adolescents. I decided to begin addressing this gap by telling my son's story. But how could this be done? The details could not be gone into. The story could not be unbearably heavy. Yet how could it not be? The story had to be honest enough to help young people think about their own loss, but not excessively confronting.

I decided to tell the story through the eyes of my son's Labrador, Baxter. A Labrador saw enough, but not too much. A Labrador can be sad and empathetic, but can also bring in enough lightness and even humour to make the story bearable. The end result, *What the Dog Saw* (Morning Star, 2017), will never be found in the children's or youth section of your local bookstore. But it is sitting on the shelves of many school counsellors, teachers, pastors and others who are finding it useful to give to children and young adults grieving a suicide. The story, while sadly true, is told by an aging Labrador, which is of course impossible. Labradors cannot manage keypads, though a few have been known to try to eat them. This is a fairly obvious example of how a book can be creative non-fiction.

Creative non-fiction is simply applying the techniques of good, interesting and creative storytelling to a non-fiction subject. This might be done in overtly imaginative ways, like having an animal as narrator, or through a combination of stylistic, structural and storytelling techniques. Perhaps the best judges of whether or not a work can be considered creative non-fiction are the readers. When the readers enjoy the book, the writing, the style, the way the story is told, and value the book for these things as well as its ability to impart information, then the author has successfully written a work of creative non-fiction.

CHAPTER 20:

Writing Biblical Fiction

'If you want to read something accurate, stick to the Bible'
– online criticism of a work of biblical fiction.

'What a trustworthy biblical novelist does is take the scripture and bring it to realistic life with layers of color and texture and sensory details. We research the historical time period ... so that we can get a feel for how people actually wrote, lived and spoke. ... We consider human nature, which does not change. People still get angry, frustrated and depressed.... But the parts that spring from our imagination, we freely admit are fiction.'
– Angela Hunt[1]

When I was young a friend of mine, a refugee from Vietnam, gave me a copy of *Barabbas* by the Swedish author Pär Lagerkvist. It had been published in 1950, and because I had grown up in the West, he assumed I had at least heard of it. But I had never before encountered anything like it. I thought characters in the Bible needed to remain in the Bible, and that we could not speculate as to what else they might have done or said, or what their motivations might have been. But here was an original and powerful novel that asked the question: What would have happened to Barabbas after his release? Would he have run and hid, or followed the crowds to witness the execution of the one who was dying in his place? Would he have spent the rest of his life fixated on who this man was and why he'd died as he did? The book awakened me to the reality that there were entire stories populated by interesting biblical characters that had never been explored.

Over the years I discovered a whole range of fiction set in biblical times and often based upon biblical characters. Some of it was by famous authors such as Thomas Mann (*Joseph and his Brothers,* in four books,

1 Angela Hunt, 'Why Biblical Fiction?' posted in *Christian Fiction*, 2 Feb. 2018. https://wwwangelahuntbooks.com/2018/02/why-biblical-fiction (accessed 24.01.2019).

1943), Norman Mailer (*The Gospel According to the Son,* 1997), Jeffrey Archer (*The Gospel According to Judas,* 2007), Anne Rice (*Christ the Lord,* in two books, 2005, 2008), Geraldine Brooks (*The Secret Chord,* 2015) and most recently Christos Tsiolkas (Damascus, 2019). Others are classics that had been successful as mainstream novels long before biblical fiction was seen as a distinct genre. These include most notably Lew Wallace's *Ben Hur: A Tale of the Christ* (1880),[2] Lloyd Douglas' *The Robe* (1942) and Nikos Kazantzakis' *The Last Temptation of Christ* (1960), all of which have been made into major motion pictures. Of course, most biblical historical fiction is by lesser-known writers, and often written out of and for a specifically religious context. The stories vary greatly in quality and intent, but together they form a unique and growing genre of literature in its own right.

Historical fiction and biblical fiction

Technically, biblical fiction is a subcategory of historical fiction. Biblical fiction is set in a certain historical time and place, and often based upon actual historical characters, such as Moses, King David, St Paul or even Jesus. All the skills needed to write historical fiction need to be brought to bear in the writing of biblical fiction. The same need for research, the same ability to give the story the feel of another time and place, the same ability to find the gaps in the existing history or story that can turn the book into an engaging and original tale, are all required. But in addition, some other skills are needed.

The writer of biblical fiction must not only be familiar with the historical period, but with the biblical context of the story. Where does the author's story fit into the larger biblical world, not only historically, but also religiously? The writer also needs some basic awareness of either Hebrew or Greek New Testament biblical studies, depending on the specific setting of the novel.

The writer of biblical fiction needs to be aware of the religious sensitivities and importance connected to various biblical accounts and characters. This is not to say that works of biblical fiction must be

2 Wallace's book, published by Harper and Brothers, remained the all-time best selling US novel until it was finally supplanted more than half a century later by Margaret Mitchell's *Gone with the Wind.*

dictated by these concerns, but to not be aware of them would be foolish. If the writer intends to challenge some common and firmly held religious conceptions, this should be done intentionally and with full knowledge of what these are, and not simply bumble into it unawares.

Also, when writing biblical fiction, the author will either be targeting a Christian audience with fixed views about many of the characters and stories, or a non-Christian or even non-religious audience more open (and perhaps even expecting) a radical revision of the accepted stories. In my experience, most works of biblical fiction are either meant to inspire the faithful, or offend the faithful. There seems to be little in between.

Sometimes, however, the faithful can be challenged to see things from a new perspective without openly confronting firmly held views. A friend of mine, Valerie Volk, did this superbly in a series of monologues by little known or peripheral biblical characters in her book *Bystanders* (Wakefield Press, 2015). Because few have any great attachment to characters such as Esau's wife, the messenger delivering notes between Joab and King David concerning Uriah the Hittite, the chariot driver of the Ethiopian Eunuch, or Paul's friend Phoebe, we are more open to hearing their view of events from the fringe.

Similarly, in a book titled *If They Could Talk: Bible Stories Told by the Animals,* edited appropriately by veterinary surgeon and writer Susan J. Bruce (Morning Star, 2018), some difficult themes are tackled by the contributors, but all stories are seen through the eyes of various animals who appear in the biblical stories. It is much easier to challenge traditional conceptions of what happened and what an event might mean when a sheep, donkey, whale or dove is telling the story.

One of the challenges of writing biblical fiction is finding the right angle or perspective. Both the above titles provide some excellent examples of how this might be done without the more obvious and risky approach, say, of telling Jesus' story from his own perspective.

If you are thinking of writing biblical fiction, consider starting out with some short stories or monologues to hone your skills. This is a good way to test the waters before plunging straight in to a major work.

Writing *Iscariot*

I had written a few short stories of biblical fiction, mostly from the perspective of the animals, and a couple from the perspective of angels. It didn't seem too hard. When I decided to write a novel based on the life of Judas, exploring some of the many questions left unanswered by the gospel accounts, I thought it would be straightforward. It turned out to be one of the most difficult writing projects I ever took on. I certainly gained a whole new level of respect for the authors of quality biblical fiction.

In the case of *Iscariot* (Morning Star, 2018) I knew early on what I wanted to achieve. But every time I completed a draft section of the novel it just didn't seem to quite work. I rewrote the novel from scratch four times, not counting the many significant revisions within these rewrites. I tried present and past tense, first-person narration and omniscient narrator. I tried multiple points of view. I tried contemporary language and language that seemed almost biblical in its formality. In retrospect, I think part of the difficulty was the subject matter. Writing a story from the perspective of a character most have learned to despise was always going to be a challenge. But there was more to it than that.

At one point in the process, frustrated that I could not find the right way to tell the story, I went through the collection of biblical fiction on my shelves and made two stacks of books. One stack consisted of those books I thought worked really well; the other of those that just didn't seem to work. The latter stack, though containing some very skilled and even well-known writers, was by far the largest. Next, I asked myself why the books in the smaller stack worked as novels, while the ones in the larger stack did not. In the end, I found there were several unique challenges involved in writing good biblical fiction, and the success of the finished books depended very much upon how successful the authors were in addressing these special difficulties.

Five unique challenges of writing biblical fiction

The first challenge was one of language. Biblical stories and characters are so well known that there are strong expectations of how the reader expects the story to be told, and how they expect the characters to sound. If the writer tries to capture too much of the biblical feel, the story ends up sounding like a lost book of the Bible. If the language is too contemporary or casual, it somehow doesn't seem to fit in biblical times. In my initial attempts at writing *Iscariot* I erred in both directions before settling upon a tone of language that I felt fit the story.

The second challenge has to do with the familiarity of the stories and characters. Everyone knows, for instance, who Jesus, Martha, John and Judas were. The story must keep the characters fresh and interesting or the reader will lose interest. But they must also remain connected enough to what we know (or believe we know) about these characters and their stories to remain credible. If the writer departs too far from these fixed views, some readers will react badly. If the writer sticks too closely to the traditional portrayals of these characters, then the resulting story is often reduced to little more than a bland retelling of the biblical account, with some extra dialogue and action thrown in to pad it out. In the writing of *Iscariot* I found this problem especially complex. Everyone knew who Judas was, and most had a profoundly negative view of him. This presented a two-fold challenge. If I presented Judas as an unlikeable and evil character, who would want to read a story about him? And why would I want to write such a story? If I presented Judas in a more human light, however, would those readers who have learned to despise Judas and his role in Jesus' death be able to think of him in this way without rebelling against what they might perceive as an unjustified rehabilitation of an evil character?

The third challenge is one of piety. If the story is being written as a homage to a particular biblical character, the character often comes across as too nice, too perfect, too uninteresting and too unbelievable. The result is simple hagiography, which is understandable given that many of the characters are literally counted as saints. But saint's stories generally exclude all the grey areas and embarrassing stuff that make for a good story, leaving us with very flat characters who sound more like something from a Sunday School lesson than a novel. On the other extreme, some writers try to make the main character or characters so different to their biblical model, and so challenging to general pious conceptions, that the characters end up being unbelievable. For this reason most novels focusing on Jesus end up either being boring retellings of gospel accounts, careful to present Jesus even more piously than the gospels themselves, or they portray a Jesus so conflicted, confused or angry that he is unrecognisable and the reader is left wondering why anyone would follow him at all.

The fourth challenge is one of passionate historical debate. There is plenty of background information available about biblical characters and events. Often too much, from the standpoint of the writer of biblical fiction. Much of the information can be contradictory, depending on the religious commitments of the scholars involved. If we write a historical novel about a person from ancient Rome or Elizabethan times, we find there is much that is agreed upon and we set our story within a context that will not ruffle the feathers of too many historians. But biblical scholars, and their readers, are a much more passionate lot. There are multiple interpretations of almost every aspect of each biblical story. It is difficult to simply set the story in a biblical background without buying into, even unintentionally, a number of theological controversies. At the very least, the writer of biblical fiction needs to be aware of these controversies. For the writer of biblical fiction, ignorance is only bliss until the reviews come in!

The fifth challenge I call 'the Jesus problem.' If a work of biblical fiction is based upon a character connected to Jesus' life, as was the case with my novel about Judas Iscariot, then the writer will soon encounter a significant quandary. Jesus does not work well as a secondary character. If he is too much in the background and unimportant, he seems unbelievable and we wonder why the main character in the story is so affected by him. If Jesus is portrayed as a charismatic and confident figure whom others gravitate toward, then he becomes a scene stealer and the character who is the centre of our story will have trouble emerging from his shadow. Additionally, if people have strong attachment to their preconceived views of biblical characters, then this phenomenon can be multiplied exponentially when it comes to Jesus. And the various pious views of Jesus are not the same. So no matter how you portray Jesus in your story, some readers are going to be left unhappy. So the writer is forced either to keep Jesus deliberately in the background, or to boldly adopt an approach as to how he will be presented and hope readers will be able to cope.

My portrayal of Jesus in *Iscariot* was fairly traditional. I was already pushing enough boundaries simply by trying to get readers to see Judas in a different light. To have an entirely new conception of Jesus as well, when it was not necessary for the main story, would have served little purpose. But even then, I have received as many complaints about my portrayal of Jesus as I have of the character of Judas – even though the novel is about Judas and told from his perspective.

Some felt my Jesus was too casual and friendly. He should have been only concerned with the business of preaching and telling the disciples how they should live. They objected that Jesus laughed and told a joke or two. There was nothing in the gospels, I was assured, about Jesus laughing. Hence it couldn't have happened. Another felt that it was okay to include Jesus in the story (it could hardly be avoided, after all) but he should have no dialogue attributed to him that was not actually in the gospels, and it should appear in exactly the form it did in the gospels. Another rang me up to say she was not happy that Jesus looked like he allowed Judas to betray him, knowing full well what the end result would be for both of them. When I asked how this was any more of a problem than the portrayal of the story in the actual gospel accounts, I was met with silence.

So, if you have Jesus in your story, even as a minor character, write his scenes carefully. You will likely have to defend them all, no matter how innocent they seemed when you wrote them.

If serious consideration is not given to each of these special problems, the novel will often flounder, leaving the author wondering just where and how they went wrong.

But despite such challenges, the effort of writing biblical fiction is well worth the while. The characters, stories and situations from the biblical accounts are strong, and there are so many unanswered questions and situations waiting to be explored. The more difficult the challenge, the greater the result when we get it right. While many works of biblical fiction are simply meant to shock, and others are sugary exercises in religious devotion, others rise above these pitfalls to become powerful stories that challenge us to rethink what we believe we know about people and events that have shaped the faith of generations.

Odds and Ends

Chapter 21:

Writer's Block

> *'To cure writer's block simply take your head and bang it on your desk until you either lose consciousness or come to grips with the fact that you, and you alone, must write the next sentence.'*
>
> – Evan Schaeffer[1]

> *'When in doubt have a man come through a door with a gun in his hand.'*
>
> – Raymond Chandler, crime fiction writer.[2]

Most writers, at some stage or another, encounter the curse of writer's block. You know you have a story in you, you may even be well into writing a novel, but then the words dry up. The harder you try to keep writing, the more difficult the task becomes. If you went to a literary doctor to see what ailed you, they would probably first check to see if your writer's block was the symptom of some underlying malady. Perhaps you have been under some extraordinary stress, perhaps you have not been feeling well, perhaps you have recently moved residences and are having difficulty adjusting to a new home or neighbourhood. If something obvious is going on that may explain your sudden inability to let the words flow, then take the time to deal with the root cause rather than continuing to stress about not being able to write. In the end, a weekend or two away may be all you need.

A writer friend of mine, who admits to suffering the occasional bout of writer's block, described the experience in verse.

---

1 Evan Schaeffer, in 'Evan Schaeffer's Legal Underground' posted Feb 09, 2015. https://www.legalunderground.com/2015/02raymond-chandlers-cure-for-writers-blick (accessed 24.1.2019).

2 Raymond Chandler, a well-known 20th-century American writer of crime fiction, gave this advice on the problem of getting stuck with a story in 'The Simple Art of Murder,' in *The Saturday Review of Literature* (April 1950).

Writer's Block

Burning, churning, wanting free,
tales and stories within me
ready to escape, to flee,
thoughts with passion bated.
Freedom grab so eagerly
Those who long have waited.

Heart is pounding, mouth so dry,
expectation souring high.
Eyes cast down where pages lie
with writer's block invaded.
Empty, white, awaiting my
words that long since faded.[3]

How to get writer's block

Perhaps your problem is very different. It might seem to you that every serious writer of note suffers from writer's block – sometimes for years. You go to workshops and conferences and hear writers you admire talk of their struggle with writer's block. You would like to join in the professional conversation, but honestly, you have never experienced the inability to put words on paper. You feel left out, as if you are missing something vital. You wonder if you are a real writer if you haven't experienced writer's block. Well, stress no more. Here are some tips for ever-flowing writers on how to experience writer's block.

1. Take on a project with an impossible deadline or a theme about which you know very little.
2. Try to work on three separate writing projects at once.
3. Go on a remote writers' retreat and bring a notebook but no pen, or your laptop but no recharger!
4. Don't start writing until at least midnight (having gotten up at 6 am).
5. Decide to write an historical novel set in a period about which you

3 Yr Ham, 'Writer's Block,' in *Tales from the Upper Room: Stores and Poetry from Tabor Adelaide's 2007 Creative Writing Programme*, ed. Claire Bell, et al. (Adelaide: Pantaenus Press, 2007), 138.

know almost nothing.

6. If male, write a book about how women think. If female, write a book about how men think.
7. Sit down with a blank piece of paper and determine to write nothing until you come up with the most perfect opening sentence for a novel ever conceived.
8. Choose an unworkable combination of any two of the above.

Overcoming writer's block

Now that you have experienced writer's block and feel like a real writer, how do you get over it?

One trick is to stop what you are doing and work on something else. You might consider taking a break from writing to do some general leisure reading, or do some background research into your novel. The problem may come down to one of performance anxiety, and the remedy is simply to start writing again – anything. A stream of consciousness exercise may be just the trick. Or perhaps you might consider continuing your story with deliberate nonsense and bad writing (to take the pressure of expectation off) until you find your writing becoming more serious again. At this point you may simply delete the nonsense you have written and pick up at the point where the words started to flow once more. Whatever you do, the important thing to remember is that writers write. They love to tell stories, to describe what they have seen or imagined. Whether you do this in a journal, a letter, or as part of your next novel, the important thing is to find a way to keep writing, to keep telling stories.

Exercise: Stream of consciousness

Take out a pen and pad of paper and go somewhere. It should be someplace relatively quiet. It might be on a bench in the city or in your local shopping centre. Start writing. Write whatever comes into your head. Write down what you are thinking, what you see, what you hear and smell. In places your writing may become very introspective, reflecting for instance on your thoughts about the exercise itself. This is okay. Everything is allowed. Simply write whatever comes into your head. Continue the exercise for about 15 minutes. You may find you have actually produced a couple of interesting sentences or observations. The main point is that you are writing, and that you are learning to put your thoughts and observations on to paper.

Chapter 22:

Rewriting and Editing

> *'To write is to rewrite. One writes for oneself, and one rewrites for others'*
>
> – Carlos Ruiz Zafón[1]

There are three different types of review a novel should undergo before being submitted for publication. These are (1) structural edit, (2) stylistic or copy edit, and (3) proofreading. Because they are often referred to both collectively and individually as 'editing', writers frequently confuse them. Sometimes a writer believes that because one of them has been done, so have the others. Sometimes a writer, in a hurry or in an effort to save money, will try to have them done simultaneously. I have often been asked something along the lines of: 'Could you please look at the structure of this novel, and while you are at it, could you point out any style issues or typos as I intend to submit it to some publishers next month.' But each of these reviews needs to take place in sequence, allowing for the writer to make the necessary revisions before proceeding to the next stage. Sometimes the whole process will need to be repeated.

Structural editing

When I was a seminary student in the early 1980s I remember having to read a particular book for homiletics class. While I have forgotten much of what was in the book, one piece of advice made a lasting impression. 'The quality of the sermon is shown,' the author said, 'by the quality of the discard heap.'[2] The advice works not just for sermons, but for any kind of writing. We must not be afraid to leave things out that we think are quite clever or well-written but don't actually progress our story. If you feel you are taking out some very good bits, then take solace in the fact that the quality of your scrap heap says a great deal about the quality

---

1 Carlos Ruiz Zafón, *The Labyrinth of the Spirits,* 790.

2 George Sweazey, *Preaching the Good News* (Englewood Cliffs, NJ: Prentice-Hall, 1976), 117.

of your final product. If you are finding it difficult to let things go from your manuscript, save these bits in a special file where you can retrieve them later to reinsert into your story if needed, or use in some other piece of writing. It is easier to make major cuts to your work if you are able to view these as 'provisional'.

When editing your novel, imagine you are a film editor who finds their final product is too long, or seems to drag in places. Brilliant films usually have very high quality deleted scenes. This process once took place in the 'cutting room' and film editors talked about the 'cutting room floor,' which is where sections of film that were literally cut from the final version ended up. A large pile of curled, discarded slices of film was a sign of a good final product. When very little was left on the cutting room floor it was either a sign that the director couldn't let anything go, or the film plot was so thin and of such poor quality that there was nothing to be cut. A similar process must take place with writing. Stephen King shared the following advice, given to him by one of his early editors: 'When you write a story, you're telling yourself the story. When you rewrite, your main job is taking out all the things that are *not* in the story.'[3]

It is one of the first and most important tasks of the writer who has finished the first draft of a novel to ask whether there are any scenes that could be shortened or are not even necessary – especially in those places where your story seems to drag on or get bogged down. Like the film director, you may occasionally decide to rearrange material, or go with a different opening scene, or an alternate ending. All these things come under the category of structural editing. They are the big questions the writer needs to ask about his or her work.

Stylistic or copyediting

Once the larger scale, structural editing has been done, it's time to look carefully at your work in terms of style. Of course, you will have checked your grammar and spelling carefully. And you will not simply have relied on your computer's spelling and grammar check program to do this. Just because your spellcheck recognises a word doesn't mean it is the word you intended to use. And remember, most computer spellcheck programs automatically revert to US spelling for each new document you create,

3 Stephen King, *On Writing*, 56.

so inconsistences in the difference in spelling between the US and other English-speaking areas may not be picked up. Once this fairly technical side of editing is done, there is the question of style. Go through your entire manuscript asking questions like: Is this the best word or phrase? Have I written as concisely and crisply as possible? Have I included words here that are not actually doing anything – that are simply going along for the ride?

Unnecessary words and phrases are left out of good writing. But what words and phrases are these? If you struggle with writing clear, crisp sentences, you need to head off to your local bookstore and buy a copy of the classic text, *The Elements of Style*, by William Strunk and E.B. White. It's not expensive, and has been helping students write clearly since Professor William Strunk first published it in 1919. In 1959 the work was revised by one of his former students, Professor E.B. White. It's a thin book (less than 100 pages) and is convincing in large part because it follows its own advice.

Until you can get your hands on a copy of Strunk and White, here are a few tips to keep in mind when writing and editing your work.

1. Avoid overuse of adjectives and adverbs. There is almost certainly nothing quite so breathtakingly and frustratingly distracting than the cumbersome and excessive use of beautifying, decorative and adorning modifiers which serve practically no functional purpose other than to make an otherwise exceedingly short, clear and precise sentence into an excruciatingly and painfully long and laborious sentence.
2. Avoid the use of often pointless and unnecessary qualifiers such as *very*, *rather*, *so*, *pretty* and *little*. In most cases all of these words can be eliminated. Perhaps it seems so very obvious, in a rather pedantic way, but this is pretty good advice and will very likely help you write a little better. If a word adds nothing to the meaning of a sentence, leave it out.
3. Avoid fancy words. Good writers have rich vocabularies at their disposal, but they do not choose words simply to impress. They choose the best and strongest word for the job. Simple and solid Anglo-Saxon words are usually best in English prose. In other words, use cow instead of bovine, farmer instead of agrarian, craftsperson instead of

artisan, Earth instead of planet, girl instead of damsel, post or mail instead of correspondence, walk instead of perambulate, brave instead of valiant, breath instead of respiration. In my seminary days I was once asked to deliver a sermon in a little, country Methodist church. I preached to a small gathering of farmers about the beautiful agrarian imagery of Jesus' parable of the vineyard workers, and what it meant to agrarians of Jesus' time and our own. I thought it was a brilliant sermon. Afterward a representative of the congregation approached me and said, 'Some of us are wondering what an "agrarian" is.' I had failed to appreciate the genuine 'agrarian' context in which I found myself, and therefore also failed to communicate effectively because I had become too enamoured of my own learning to simply use the word 'farmers'.

4. Avoid clichés and figures of speech. It's an old saying, tried and true, but still, you can't go past the advice that your prose needs clichés and figures of speech as much as you need another hole in your head.
5. Short, to the point sentences are good prose. In primary school young writers are taught to compose complex sentences as a way of getting the student past the 'See Spot run. See Spot chase the ball' phase of writing. But once we have learned that Spot can both run and chase the ball in the same sentence, there is a danger that we make a virtue out of ever longer and more complex sentences. The following ninety-six word gem with fourteen commas and two semi-colons was produced by Charles Dickens. Such lengthy sentences were not uncommon for the day, though in the hands of lesser writers the results are frequently even more painful.

> In a preposterous coat, like a beadle's, with cuffs and flaps exaggerated to an unspeakable extent; in an immense waistcoat, knee-breeches, buckled shoes, and a mad cocked hat, with nothing fitting him, and everything of coarse material, moth-eaten, and full of holes; with seams in his black face, where fear and heat had started through the greasy composition daubed all over it, any living thing so grimly, detestably, ridiculously shameful as the whelp in his comic livery Mr. Gradgrind never could by any other means have believed in, weighable and measurable fact though it was.[4]

4 Charles Dickens. *Hard Times*, in *The Great Masters Library* (New York: Chatham River Press, 1986), 520.

If a sentence can be clearly divided into two or three crisp and easy to read sentences, then divide it. The full stop is your friend. Use it.

1. Write clearly. If you find a sentence that is not clear, revise it. As Strunk and White put it:

> When you become hopelessly mired in a sentence, it is best to start fresh; do not try to fight your way through against the terrible odds of syntax . . . . Muddiness is not merely a disturber of prose, it is also a destroyer of life, of hope: death on the highway caused by a badly worded road sign, heartbreak among lovers caused by a misplaced phrase in a well-intentioned letter, anguish of a traveler expecting to be met at a railroad station and not being met because of a slipshod telegram.

2. Finally, be concise. Clarity and concision go hand in hand. I like to think that I write concisely. Several years ago I wrote a short story for a competition that had a maximum limit of 1000 words. When I finished my story and checked my word count I had written 1250 words. Worse yet, the story had to be submitted later that afternoon! I went back through the story three times, cutting every unnecessary word until I had brought the word count down to 998. The thing that struck me afterward was that the story not only read better, but also, I couldn't remember most of the things I had taken out. I wondered what those other 252 words had been doing in the story in the first place.

Proofreading

Proofreading is not editing. Proofreading is looking for and correcting typos, misspellings and incorrect punctuation. But many good proofreaders, especially if it is a friend or collegue helping you out, will also make editorial suggestions and comments along the way. This is fine, but it does not belong properly to the task at hand. Proofreading, especially if you are paying someone to do this for you, should be done at the end of the process, after all changes and revisions have been made to your manuscript. If you have your manuscript proofread too early, then continue to make significant changes, you will need to have the entire thing corrected again.

Before sending off your manuscript to be proofread, go over it as thoroughly as you can yourself. The cleaner your manuscript, the more your proofreader will be able to see and correct. You do not want them to spend all of their time finding things you could have found on your own if you had made the effort – especially if you are paying them by the hour. You also do not want to make it difficult to find the hard to spot issues simply because there are so many obvious ones cluttering every page.

Some authors like to do their own corrections and leave it at that. This is especially true of those who have the skills and training to do this. But even if you proofread for others, you should still have someone else go over your own manuscript at the end of the process. No matter how good you are at correcting text, the reality is that you are more likely to miss mistakes in your own writing than you would be in someone else's. The reason for this is simple. You know what you meant to say, and when you read it, that is what you see and hear. I have carefully read some chapters in my manuscripts dozens of times, and am always shocked by how many obvious mistakes – mistakes I would have immediately picked up in anyone else's writing – were sitting there all along, and were identified by my proofreader.

Choose your proofreader(s) well. Many are happy to go with a friend who is good at grammar and will do it for free. This is fine if they are actually good at their task. But being well-read and good with grammar are not enough. Of course, you want a proofreader who actually understands the finer points of spelling, grammar and punctuation. But you also want someone who has a meticulous eye for picking these things up. Not everyone can do this. If you suspect your proofreader is overly pedantic, probably suffering from OCD, and is likely somewhere on the spectrum, all the better. They might have their issues, but they probably possess just the skills you desperately need!

Beta readers

All the rage of late is beta readers. A *beta reader* simply refers to a non-professional reader, especially one who is part of your target audience. These are often friends or acquaintances who are happy to read your manuscript, point out any problems, and tell you what they thought of the story. The main value of beta readers is that they can give you an idea of how target-audience readers are likely to react to your work. They are very useful if you can find good ones. And they work for free simply for the love of literature, or because of their friendship with you. But they are not professional editors. Sending off your 'finished' manuscript to a group of trusted beta readers is a great idea. But do not make the mistake of thinking that your novel has thereby been professionally edited and proofread. It has not.

Working with an editor

Writers are very funny about working with an editor, whether it is a friend, a fellow writer, a mentor, or a paid editor. Some writers feel that if they get any help or assistance, then the work is not their own. They feel that they are somehow a fraud or a cheat, exposed like some fallen cycling or track star caught using performance-enhancing drugs. I have experienced this resistance to working with an editor from both sides of the process. As a supervisor of a number of MAs in creative writing, and as an editor with a publisher, I have found that even the best of writers naturally cringe at the thought of being edited. Some fear they will be told their work is no good, others fear their work will be changed or altered from the state of inspired narration they achieved over several late nights, others still seem to genuinely think that any sentence improved through the insights of a good editor is somehow no longer their sentence. But good writing is seldom produced without going through a long and even tedious process of revision and rewriting. Working with one or more editors is often a crucial part of this process.

As a writer, I know it is not easy being edited. When I give my work to a writing colleague, or proofreader, or publishing editor, I always hope they will get back to me saying something like: 'This is pure genius. It is beautiful language. I could not find anything to change apart from a few unnecessary commas. Well done, thou good and faithful writer, please enter into the halls of literary greatness.'

Of course, no one ever says this. And if they did, it would be of little benefit to anything other than my ego. The truth is, when the pages come back thoroughly marked with questions, suggestions and corrections, I know that after I work through these, taking many on board, my manuscript will be much improved from what I began with. But the experience is often painful. One of the best descriptions of what it feels like to be edited comes from a wonderful novel by the Spanish writer Carlos Ruiz Zafón. His fictional writer (a slightly veiled version of himself) sought the help of an experienced writer, the fictional Julian Carax, in producing his first novel. Zafón writes:

> Every time we met, Carax went carefully through the new pages I handed him. He pulled his pen open and made notes that he would then use to point out, with endless patience, what I'd done wrong, which was almost everything. Point by point he would show me what didn't work, giving me the reason why and explaining in detail how it could be fixed. His analysis was extraordinarily meticulous. For every error I thought I'd made, he'd show me fifteen whose existence I hadn't even suspected. He pulled apart every word, every sentence and every paragraph, and put them back together again like a goldsmith working with a magnifying glass. He did all this without condescension, as if he were an engineer telling an apprentice how combustion or steam engines work. Sometimes he would question turns of phrase and ideas that I thought were the only things likely to be saved that day.[5]

Being edited is a difficult process for any writer. If you are fortunate enough to find someone like Zafón's fictional Julian Carax, then thank your lucky, literary stars. Do not run from them in fear or resent them. Embrace what they can offer. Take heart in the knowledge that a careful reader thinks your work merits their detailed attention. But in the end, you are the writer. You should only make those changes that you are finally convinced improve the work. Never make a change because someone else insists that it is an improvement. You must be convinced yourself. Sometimes you might only be persuaded that what you had written does not quite work, but you are not convinced that the suggested change works either. The whole process drives you to find another solution. In this way progress is made; in this way, mediocre manuscripts become good novels.

---

5 Carlos Ruiz Zafón. *The Labyrinth of the Spirits*, 789.

CHAPTER 23:

Grammar Matters

'Ego sum rex Romanus, et supra grammaticam'

– Emperor Sigismund at the Council of Constance, 1414.

'That sure is a great school. It's practical. They don't teach no damn grammar there.'

– Kansas farmer, 1915.

Despite the views expressed in these quotes, grammar does matter. We might not understand it, we might dislike the idea of it, but we all use it. Even Emperor Sigismund could not have proclaimed himself to be above grammar without following certain grammatical conventions to make himself understood. And the Kansas farmer from over a century ago may not have liked grammar, but with three short, succinct sentences, each with subject, object and verb, he made his point very clear, thanks to grammar. So, what exactly is grammar, and why is it so important?

Language and the imago dei

The fundamental difference between human and all other creatures' forms of communication, according to ethologists specialising in language research, is grammar.[1] Many species can communicate danger, fear, concern, aggression, interest in mating and location of food sources – but only human beings link concepts and thoughts together in complex relationships in our communication with one another. From a philosophical point of view, grammar is vitally important to our humanity. It is therefore also significant for a Christian understanding of the *imago dei*. If we reflect the image of God primarily in a relational way, then human language, with its necessary in-built grammar, is an important facilitator of all communication-orientated relationships.

1 Cf. Mark Worthing Worthing, "Human and Animal Intelligence: A Difference of Degree or Kind?" in *God, Life, Intelligence and the Universe*, J. Puddefoot, A. Foerst and M. Worthing. (Adelaide: ATF Press, 2002), 99ff.

Without grammar there would be no language. Without language there would be no community.

When we think of grammar, however, we tend to think not so much of the basic relationships between the symbols we use to communicate as we do the 'rules' which govern these relationships.

What is grammar?

Various definitions exist for what we commonly refer to as grammar. In the most general sense, grammar is 'the total set of signals by which a given language expresses its meaning.'[2] More specifically and technically, former *London Times* editor Philip Howard defined grammar as that 'branch of linguistics that deals with a language's inflexions (accidence), other structures of words (morphology), its phonetics system (phonology), and the arrangement of its words in sentences (syntax)'[3] Perhaps more simply, we might say that grammar describes the relationships between words that make effective and complex human communication possible.

Function of grammar: Prescriptive versus descriptive grammars

An example of a prescriptive grammar is H. Marmaduke Hewitt's *A Manual of Our Mother Tongue* from the late nineteenth century. Under this approach the rules of English usage are set out and examples of errors are sought, wherever they might be found, so that they may be corrected. In Hewitt's collection of examples of bad grammar, he includes Milton, Shakespeare and Dickens! Even those grammar books not so prone to this sort of presumption took the prescriptive approach in this era. For instance, Percival Leigh's singular *The Comic English Grammar* explains its purpose thus: 'As Spartans used to exhibit a tipsy slave to their children with a view to disgust them with drunkenness, so we, by giving a few examples here and there, of incorrect phraseology, shall expose, in their naked deformity, the vices of speech to the ingenuous reader.'[4] As one might expect, there was not a lot that was humorous

2 Roberts, Paul. *Understanding English* (New York: Harper, 1958), 132.

3 Howard, Philip. *The State of the Language. English Observed* (London: Hamish Hamilton, 1984), 119.

4 Leigh, Percival. *The Comic English Grammar. An Introduction to the English Tongue.* (London: Richard Bentley, 1840), ix,x.

about *The Comic English Grammar* of 1840, as it was those who spoke 'incorrectly' who were ridiculed, rather than the grammarians and their often pretentious rules.

By contrast, the descriptive approach to grammar looks to examples, usually among contemporary users, to show how the language is actually spoken. Such grammar books do not tell us how we should construct our phrases and sentences, but how effective writers and speakers actually do construct them. The current trend is clearly in the direction of a descriptive approach to grammar. But there is still room for a prescriptive function of grammar. Sometimes it is important for someone to adjudicate, like a referee in a football match, and say what is correct and what is not.

Grammatical disputes

With all the fastidiousness of the prescriptive school of grammarians, we might rightly wonder to what extent they agree among themselves. The reality is that there is an amazingly wide divergence of opinion on most points of usage. This then begs the question: Do the prescriptive grammarians actually know what is the correct usage?

The following dispute between two Cambridge dons was carried out via the letters to the editor section of *The Times* in February 1933 and was provoked by the alleged use of the phrase 'to try out' by the Chancellor of the university, Mr Baldwin. In response, Dr T. R. Glover, University Orator, wrote the following:

> Sir,
>
> 'In order to try out the possibilities of these new methods' – did Mr Baldwin really say that at Cambridge on Friday? I cannot believe that you would put an Americanism into his mouth. . . . Am I to take it that the Chancellor admitted this phrase, as it were, to an honorary degree? 'To try out' – are we to accept it as English, and Cambridge? Out upon him!
>
> Do you notice how 'out' creeps in? St Paul long ago told us to work out our salvation; endless people tell us to look out; 'little orphant Annie' warned us that 'the goblins will get you if you don't watch

> out.' When Professor Kapitza and his staff have 'tried out' their methods, does Mr Baldwin expect them to 'win out' or to 'lose out'? I respectfully hope neither. ….
>
> Yours, etc.,
>
> T.R. Glover[5]

It was quite a shot across the bow for the poor Chancellor, who was, after all, only trying out a phrase. But the whole debate played out in a rather unexpected way, leaving Dr Glover on the outer. The following day a letter appeared by Prof Ernest Barker, also of Cambridge, who pointed out what many today still fail to recognise; namely, that many so-called American corruptions are actually older forms of British dialect abandoned by the educated elite, but carried to America by the common folk who still employ them. Wrote Prof Barker:

> Sir,
>
> Dr Glover gambols humorously in regard to American prepositions. But is he not, in this matter of 'try out', mounted upon the wrong elephant?
>
> To 'try out' is to refine and to purify the good stuff of a metal from the clinging dross. The term is of Biblical and Tudor English, as other 'Americanisms' sometimes are. *The New English Dictionary* cites the Great Bible of 1539: 'Examen me, O Lord, & prove me; trie out my reynes and my hert.' When Mr Baldwin spoke of 'trying out the possibilities of new methods', he used an apposite metaphor and a piece of fine Old English.
>
> I am, Sir, your obedient servant,
>
> Ernest Barker

History of grammar

Grammar is as old as human language. Whether it is understood, analysed or not, grammar simply is. Its rejection and disparagement, following the best grammatical forms, cannot dissolve it into non-existence. Whenever people use any kind of language to communicate with one another, grammar is at work.

5 For this and the following see Gregory, Kenneth, ed. *The Second Cuckoo. A New Selection of Letters to the Times since 1900* (Falmouth, Cornwall: Unwin, n.d.)

But at what point did human beings begin to self-consciously analyse the grammar of their languages? This honour would seem to belong first to the Greeks and then to the Romans, both of whom taught children grammar in schools and wrote treatises, often under the category of rhetoric, exploring its intricacies. Other earlier societies may have made steps in this direction, but we have no records of it, and it is the work of the Greeks and Romans which has provided much of the framework and vocabulary for our own modern teaching and analysis of grammar.

History of English grammar

The study of English grammar is a relatively recent phenomenon. The grammar schools of old were so named for their study of Latin, not English grammar.

The general growth of interest in English as a language in the mid-eighteenth century, expressed in such milestones as the appearance of Samuel Johnson's dictionary in 1755, also brought with it an interest in the study of English grammar. But the early grammar books of this period were essentially Latin grammars superimposed upon English. This tendency remained predominant among grammars up to the mid-twentieth century. My own university grammar text (from the 1980s) was of this ilk. We were required to read George Curme's 1925 *College English Grammar* not so we could better write and understand English, but as pre-requisite for the study of classical languages.

In the 1960s a new generation of grammarians began to do two very radial things. Firstly, they argued that their function was not to police the way the language was spoken, but rather to describe the way it was spoken. And secondly, they began to change the terminology describing various grammatical functions from the traditional Latin categories to words more descriptive and representative of modern English. Both of these shifts in thinking are still in progress, but on balance seem to have won the day among experts in the field. The trickle-down effect, benefiting the hordes of grammar teachers and self-appointed guardians of the language, however, lingers somewhat behind.

Today, particularly in primary and secondary educational settings, some have nearly abandoned the teaching of grammar altogether. What are the positive and negative consequences of this move? Is there still any point in learning grammar if so few appear to be taking it seriously? Again, whether grammar is taught or not, it is still there. People still struggle to understand poorly constructed sentences. Speakers and writers of English do themselves a grave disservice by dismissing the importance of learning grammar. And this is nowhere more true than for the aspiring writer, who hopes to make his or her way in the world through the medium of written language.

Why learn grammar?

One grammarian assessed the damage done to grammar's reputation well:

> The most damaging thing that can be said about English grammars … is not that they are useless but that they are essentially untrue. Study of them yields no intellectual satisfaction. It is probably this rather than their asserted uselessness which has led to the decline of the study of grammar in modern times. Students and teachers alike have rebelled against having to seek understanding of something which was not ultimately understandable.[6]

So why learn grammar? It is easy to climb aboard the anti-grammar bandwagon, but there are some compelling reasons for studying grammar.

1. Human language is vital to our humanity and our culture. Understanding how our own language and other languages work, regardless how difficult at times, is a worthwhile pursuit in its own right.
2. People who do not learn grammar are typically unable to write well. If you wish to write, and to write clearly, the study of grammar simply cannot be avoided.
3. While some people simply seem to have a feel for what sounds right in a sentence, many are only able to acquire this skill through the study of grammar; that is, by learning the 'rules'.
4. For those learning English, or any other language as a second language, study and understanding of the grammar of the language is usually indispensable for a mastery of the language.
5. For writers, if you do not have a sound understanding of the grammar

6 Roberts, Paul. *Understanding English* (New York: Harper, 1958), 141f.

of your own language, you will be greatly limited in what you are able to do with that language. Your writing will suffer from unnecessary lack of clarity, and editors and publishers looking at your manuscript will spot the deficiencies immediately and wonder what kind of author gives so little attention to the construction of the language in which they write.

6. Finally, if you are a genuine grammatical rebel, wanting to break the rules in your writing to make a point, you can do this convincingly and effectively only if you understand what these 'rules' or conventions actually are.

Can I improve my grammar?

'Okay,' you say, 'I am convinced that grammar is important. But after never learning it properly, and ignoring it for so long, can anything be done now to improve my grammar?'

The answer, of course, is yes. First of all, you need to recognise that you already understand a good deal of grammar. You might not know what certain functions are called, but you know when something doesn't sound right. So take heart, you are not starting out from zero.

Firstly, I would suggest buying a couple of good readable books on grammar. Don't buy the advanced guides for English lecturers and professional editors. They will leave you feeling overwhelmed. Buy something like *English Grammar for Dummies* by Wendy Anderson, Geraldine Woods and Lesley Ward.[7] And if you don't mind the insinuation of this first title, you might also consider Laurie Rozakis' *The Complete Idiot's Guide to Grammar and Style.*[8] Try to ensure that at least one of your grammar books is Australian (or at least British), as American English grammar differs in a few places from Australian and British usage. Also, if English is not your first language, look for a good ESL English grammar as well. The reason for buying at least two basic books on grammar is so that if one author's way of explaining something is not making sense to you, you can cross check it in another book.

7 2nd Australian ed. John Wiley and Sons Australia, 2012.

8 New York: Penguin Group, 2003.

Secondly, whenever anyone corrects your writing, ask them why they made certain changes. Make it a policy never to accept a correction until you understand the reason for it. You will be surprised how quickly you will improve your ability to self-edit your own work when you begin to understand the sort of mistakes you are prone to make and how to fix them.

Finally, don't give up. Your usage will improve. Don't worry if you feel you are still making many mistakes. Grammar, after all, is meant to describe how real people actually speak and write. It is not meant to stop you from writing until such time as you have mastered all the 'rules'. We learn grammar to improve our writing. Grammar serves writing, not the other way around. Do not let feelings of inadequacy in the areas of grammar and punctuation stop you from writing. The more you write, the more the quality and consistency of your language usage will improve.

Exercise: Testing grammar

Go online and find a grammar test. Something at about Year 7 level is probably a good place to start. Take the test and see how you do. Many sites will score your test automatically. Make a note of what you got wrong and use your grammar books, online resources, or check with friends to work out why you got some answers wrong. Once you feel you understood where mistakes were made, go back on online, find another test at a similar level, and repeat the process. You will be surprised how quickly your basic grammar skills will progress in this way.

Chapter 24:

Getting Published

'The search for fame and fortune are not good reasons for getting published, mainly because publication seldom brings either.'

– Kate Grenville[1]

'Do you ever read the magazines, Mr Bohlen?'

'You'll pardon me, Knipe, but what's all this got to do with your machine?'

'Everything, Mr Bohlen, absolutely everything! What I want to tell you is, I've made a study of magazines, and it seems that each one tends to have its own particular type of story. The writers – the successful ones – know this, and they write accordingly.' . . .

'My dear boy, it can't possibly be a commercial proposition – ever. You know as well as I do what it costs to build one of these machines.'

'Yes, sir, I do. But with due respect, I don't believe you know what the magazines pay writers for stories.'

'What do they pay?'

'Anything up to twenty-five hundred dollars. It probably averages around a thousand.'

Mr Bohlen jumped.

'Yes, sir, it's true.'

'Absolutely impossible, Knipe! Ridiculous!'

'No, sir, it's true.'

'You mean to sit there and tell me that these magazines pay out money like that to a man for . . . just for scribbling off

1 Kate Grenville, *The Writing Book*, 186.

> a story! Good heavens, Knipe! Whatever next! Writers must all be millionaires!'
>
> 'That's exactly it, Mr Bohlen!'[2]

Clearly, the dialogue cited above is from a piece of fictional writing – and from the 1950s at that! The author, Roald Dahl, is having fun spoofing his own profession. But there is still an impression in some circles that writing is a good way to make one's fortune. Certainly a few high profile writers have done very well with writing. But most professional writers I know count on a combination of government subsidies for low income earners, their partner's income, and part-time work to make ends meet. If your goal is to become rich, and writing is simply your means, you have definitely chosen the wrong field. But if writing is something you feel you just have to do, then publishing – and ultimately getting some financial remuneration for your efforts – is something you must always set your sights upon.

While many write for personal enjoyment, every writer aspires to see their work in print at some stage. Once you have mastered some basic writing skills – and hopefully produced a few good pieces of prose and poetry along the way – the time will come to think about getting your work in print. Many inexperienced writers send their freshly written manuscript (usually in the wrong format and unannounced) off to the biggest publisher they can find, and watch the post (or email) for their acceptance letter and contract – neither of which, of course, ever come. This is often followed by giving up in despair. But the failure to immediately attract the interest of a major publisher does not mean that your work is no good. It is more likely the case that you are going about getting published in the wrong way and in the wrong places.

For those serious about pursuing publication there are a number of books, articles, workshops and other resources available to help you along the way. It is important that you send out the best product you can. Do not send your rough manuscript off to a publisher hoping they will see its inherent potential and genius and agree to edit it for you.

2 Roald Dahl, 'The Great Automatic Grammatizator,' [1954], in Dahl, *The Great Automatic Grammatizator and Other Stories* (London: Puffin Books, 2001), 11f. Notice Dahl's effective use of dialogue without a single 'he said/she said' or variation of same.

Revise and edit your story, poem or novel until it is in the best possible condition, then have one or two other competent readers critique and edit it as well. You will be surprised what you have missed. Only when you feel your work is in the best shape you can get it in should you send it off. Never submit a piece of writing with a covering letter that says something like: 'I know there is still heaps of work to be done on my manuscript, but I thought I would send it to you to see whether you may be interested in publishing it.' No editor wants to read a manuscript that the writer admits is still not properly revised and finished.

Also, avoid the trap of focusing all your energy on getting a novel published by a major publisher. Start small and gain experience. Send off your poetry and/or short stories to magazines and journals. Also, there is nothing wrong with sending off appropriate pieces to your congregation's or sporting club's monthly newsletter. Most creative writing programs produce an annual anthology of the best short stories and poetry from current and past students. If you are part of a creative writing course submit your best efforts for inclusion. These things might seem like small steps, but they all count as genuine publications, and when writing your author profile for future publishers, will show that you are serious about getting published and that others have found your work of suitable quality for publication.

And, of course, do not give up. It is well known in the publishing world that J.K. Rowling's first *Harry Potter* manuscript was rejected by numerous publishers before someone finally said yes. Obviously there are quite a few red-faced and regretful publishers out there now. Imagine if she had just given up after the first dozen rejections. If you believe you have produced something of quality, do not give up. Do not be discouraged by a few rejection letters – or even a whole pile of them.

One of my old creative writing teachers, S.S. Hanna, from Geneva College, Beaver Falls, Pennsylvania, had written a little novel based on his own experience of how hard it was for young academics in the early 1980s to find work. What he didn't bargain on was that it would prove even more difficult finding a publisher. After a while he became fascinated with the various kinds of rejection letters he received and began appending them (with commentary) to his book. He continued to receive rejection letters, but editors became a lot more careful about what they wrote, realising that sooner or later, with this author's persistence, he would find a publisher. In the end, the original novel had to be shortened so that there would be room for the rather comprehensive collection of rejection letters. And yes, about a year after I had him as a lecturer, Dr Hanna did finally get published (*The Gypsy Scholar*, Iowa State University Press, 1987). Although the style of letters may have changed somewhat, and many are now sent via email, I still find his collection of rejection letters and commentary on them one of the most intriguing and informative studies of an author's search for a publisher. Importantly, not all rejection letters need be discouraging. Many publishers actually liked his book, but it didn't suit the needs of their publishing house. Some offered suggestions for revision, which the author took on board. In the end, after writing to nearly every small press and university press in America, his persistence paid off.

Types of publishing

In many ways getting published today is more difficult, with fewer large players fighting over a limited number of high-profile authors. But in other respects it is also easier to be published now than it was even a decade or two ago. The general abandonment of small-scale print runs by the big publishers over the past two decades has created room for a number of small presses, many of which are willing to take a chance on new authors. Also, print-on-demand (POD) publishing has eliminated the concern over small print runs and where to store boxes of books while waiting to sell them. This, in turn, has made self-publication a realistic option for many. Coupled with the availability of quality publishing programs on home computers, a knowledgeable writer can now produce and market (on a small-scale at least) a decent quality product. But the dream and aim of most writers is still to land a contract with a major publishing house, though this in itself is no guarantee of publishing success.

Publishing options for writers today:

The major publishing house. These are publishers with actual buildings and multiple staff! They have separate people specialising in editing, proofreading, cover design, marketing and the like. They often only do large print runs, say of at least 10 000 (and often more). They are difficult to break into unless you are already an established and proven writer (i.e., you can sell books) or if you have a well-known name or story to tell.

The small publisher. These operate like the large publishers but on a much smaller scale. They often deal in print runs of 1 000 to 5 000 books, or use a print-on-demand option. They usually have a small staff with many roles being filled by part-timers. Their cover designer might also double as their promotions officer, and they will rely heavily on the author to organise promotion of their own book. But, like the large publishers, they cover the costs of cover design, typesetting, basic promotion and the like, and pay the same rates for royalties (usually 10% of sales income). Like the major publishing houses, small publishers still fall under the category of 'traditional' publishing

Subsidised publishing. These are often small publishers that survive in part or entirely by covering a portion of their costs through author contributions. Often this is in the form of requiring the author to buy a set number of books at wholesale cost (which the author is then expected to on-sell themselves at various book events and to friends and family). I have seen these arrangements go from a requirement of purchasing 100 books up to 2 000. The publisher is thus guaranteed to not lose money, and the author, if they believe strongly enough in their book, is able to back it themselves. For the most part only books that are of high enough quality are accepted, and the publisher also actively promotes the book (rather than simply listing it on their website).

Fully supported or 'vanity' publishing. When 'subsidised' publishing is entirely covered by the author, including all costs of editing, cover design and typesetting, and no manuscripts seem ever to be turned away, and no effort made to promote or sell books other that listing them on the publisher's website, then it is clear that the publishing firm is relying entirely on author payments for their income. This type of publishing is called vanity publishing because any author desperate enough to get published can pay to have this done, with little or no chance of being rejected so long as they have the money. There are not as many vanity publishers as there once were, as the astute author desperate for a publisher soon finds they can achieve the same or better result for less outlay of funds through self-publishing.

Self-publishing. When the author becomes the publisher of their own book we call this self-publishing. Often a press name is registered so that the work does not look self-published, and a website created where the book can be ordered. The author, along with their family and friends, do the editing, cover design, typesetting and web page, then send the manuscript to a printer or a print-on-demand company and order copies to sell. Self-published books vary from the overtly amateur and awful, to those (by far the minority) that are quite impressive and make strong contributions to the indie publishing scene. For some, self-publishing is the new vanity publishing. For others, it is the ultimate expression of high-quality independent publishing. If you are going to self-publish, ensure that you do it well. Your work should be properly edited and typeset. Make sure you obtain good cover design and get some advice about marketing. If these things are not well within your current capacity, but you would still like to self-publish, you might want to consider assisted self-publishing.

Hybrid publishing. Increasingly the term hybrid publishing is used. With the variety of publishing options that now exist, many publishers offer more than one type of publishing arrangement. For instance, they may operate as a small, traditional publisher, but also offer subsidized or assisted self-publishing as well. Publishers offering a range of options, or levels of publishing, are often known as hybrid publishers.

Assisted self-publishing. Self-publishing can be more difficult than it seems, and many self-published books are of poor production quality and are obviously self-published because the author did not have the necessary experience in the areas of editing, layout, typesetting and cover design. The common tip-offs are when the print is small and close together and there are almost no margins at the sides of the page (in an effort to save pages and money), the cover looks either home-made or taken off a free website, the publication page is unprofessional and includes lots of threats and warnings about copyright, the publisher's name and the author's name are the same, or the publisher has no other authors listed on their website – if it even has one – and a quick glance at the first few pages indicates that no one has properly proofread the text.

To avoid this situation, there are a number of people who are very good at producing high quality self-published works and for a fee (often quite reasonable) will do all the bits the author cannot. They will produce a good cover, typeset the work, and even provide a publishing name (often the name of their business), but they usually ask the author to ensure that the book has been properly edited and proofread. If you are looking at self-publishing and do not have the skills and experience to do this well, you are probably better off going with assisted self-publishing. You should check the quality of other books the person or group have done before signing on. Also, check that they have their own online ordering system so that readers can go through them to order books. You do not want to be posting books around the country one copy at a time for the next three years. You will also need to understand that any marketing that occurs will be entirely up to you, and that few bookstores will carry your work, or newspapers review it, as they will still view it as self-published. Your local bookstore and newspaper, however, (especially in regional towns and rural communities) are an exception. You should not be shy about approaching them as a local author to sell or review your book. Most will be more than happy to do so.

e-publishing. This has been the big and much anticipated change in book publishing since the turn of the century. The reality is that it has not taken over the industry as once expected and there are few who now expect it will any time soon. Nevertheless, it is still a viable form of publishing and many books are published solely in electronic format either through publishers or through self-publication. In most cases, however, e-publishing is done in addition to traditional hard-copy publication. For most works published in both formats, the lion's share of sales are in the area of traditional books. The Graeme Clark biography I did through Allen & Unwin in 2015, for instance, ended up with total sales of just over 10 000, only about 300 of which were e-books. That's about three percent, which is not all that uncommon. Hence the increasing reluctance of many publishers, especially smaller ones, to produce e-versions of their stock. The sometimes impressive numbers for total sales of e-books has much to do with the many thousands of authors who cannot find a publisher for their work so produce only an e-book version for sale.

Tips for manuscript submission

After having spent a few year's sitting on the other side of the publisher's desk, my advice is somewhat different, and blunter, than it would have been when most of my knowledge came from the author's side of the equation. As an author, you assume everyone else submitting manuscripts knows exactly what they are doing and have put a great deal of time into their presentation. For the most part, they do not, and they have not. So there is a real opportunity to raise your manuscript to the top of the pile when submitting to a publisher, or to a literary agent, simply by following some basic 'rules'.

1. Unless given the green light to do so, do not send in your entire manuscript, even in electronic form, with your initial approach. The first one to three chapters (depending upon their length) is plenty.
2. Your manuscript should be double spaced and justified at the left-hand margin only. Do not try to make it look like a book by justifying both margins, adding chapter and title headers and the like.
3. Include page numbers!
4. Include a short cover letter or email saying who you are, what your book is about, and thanking the person to whom you are sending it for taking the time to look at it. If possible, find the name of the editor in charge of your type of book on the publisher's website and address the letter to them personally. 'Dear editor' should be used only when no clear person responsible can be identified.
5. Include a brief (no more than one page) author bio as a separate attachment or document. Remember, this is an *author* bio. Talk about your writing training and experience, or your life and work experiences that have qualified you to write this particular book. For instance, it is very relevant if a crime novel is written by someone with police or forensic crime scene experience. But if you have written a romantic comedy, the fact that you have twenty-years' experience in law enforcement is not particularly relevant.
6. Do not try to sell your book by listing all your friends and relatives who have read and liked it, or by assuring the editor that it is a great read and will sell very well. It is their job to make that assessment. If you try to pre-empt this you will come across as amateur and insecure.

7. Do not feel that you need to send off your manuscript to only one publisher or literary agent at time, and then wait for months for a reply before trying another source. You will spend a lifetime just sending out the one manuscript. Pick a handful of first-choice options and send it out. After a couple of months feel free to send it out to anyone who might possibly be interested. The only exception to this is if a publisher has specifically asked for your manuscript. In this case, you know they want to seriously look at it, and protocol suggests you should give them this chance before sending your manuscript off to other publishers.
8. Ensure your manuscript is properly formatted. If there are formatting and style guidelines given by the publisher on their website, make sure you adapt your manuscript to these before sending it off. If none are given, go with any standard formatting and style guide. The bottom line is that your manuscript should be consistent and look professional in its formatting and style. To do otherwise is like going on a first date in your gardening clothes and then wondering why you didn't make a good impression.
9. Make sure that your manuscript is carefully proofread. It may sound incredible, but I receive a number of manuscripts each year that are clearly very poorly proofread. When I point this out to the authors who submitted them, they invariably indicate that they thought their story was so good that it was enough for me to see how well it would sell and that I would take it from there and clean it up. It is true that editors will always seek to tidy up manuscripts even further before publication, but no one appreciates being sent a substandard manuscript by an author who believes they are too important to waste time on these details. Not even successful, well-known authors do this. That's part of the reason they got to where they are in the first place. They take pride in each step of the process and would be horrified to send off a manuscript that is not as clean as they are able to get it.
10. Many publishers say they do not accept unsolicited manuscripts. Some, however, especially smaller ones, do look at those that come in. And some publishers have certain windows of opportunity in which they accept unsolicited manuscripts or book proposals. For this reason it is important to check publishers' websites carefully. The

ubiquitous statement that they do not accept unsolicited manuscripts safeguards them against a flood of poor quality manuscripts coming in, and also relieves them of the obligation of replying to each one of these. In reality, you are not risking much by sending in a query with a sample chapter attached. No one will blame you for trying, and your name is not added to a black list shared among other publishers! The worst, and most likely thing that will happen is nothing. And who knows, someone might just take a second look at your proposal.

Religious versus mainstream publishers

Many authors ask whether getting published by a religious press is easier than getting a contract with a mainstream press? In short, it is neither more nor less difficult. The same general commercial restraints and processes apply. But there are a few differences. Unlike the mainstream presses, there are fewer mega-publishers. Also, most religious presses are by definition niche publishers and will be looking at very specific markets. If your book fits into their niche market, it can make things less complicated from a publisher's standpoint. But even in the world of religious publishing, competition is stiff, and there are far more writers submitting manuscripts than there are publication slots. A religious publisher might also feel obliged to turn down a manuscript if it contains views or themes that could cause offense among their core market. So the writer needs to be aware of these sensitivities. By the same token, a Christian publisher will not feel obliged to publish your work simply because it is 'pious' or embodies the worldview or theology which they also accept. Your work still has to be good, and marketable.

The 'official' path to publication

If you are serious about getting published by a major press, or at least a significant smaller publisher, there is a semi-official process that has evolved in recent years that many follow. The path is long, will take much effort, and involves some financial investment. And there are many steps along the way where you might come to grief. But if you wonder how to progress your manuscript the official way, the process goes something like this: (1) write your manuscript. And if you have done so with the help of a creative writing course, workshop or mentor, all the better; (2) have friends who are good readers or even writers critique your manuscript; (3) revise your manuscript on the basis of comments received; (4) send your manuscript to a professional manuscript accessor. This will cost a bit, but you will receive an official assessment report back; (5) revise your manuscript in light of the report; (6) send off your revised manuscript along with the assessor's report to a literary agent or agents. You will also need to send your author bio and a letter of introduction. Many agents will not look at your manuscript unless it comes with a professional assessment report; (7) if an agent accepts you as a client, usually in return for 10% of all profits you make from your book, they will try to find a publisher for you. Most major publishers will only take manuscripts received from agents. But this is no guarantee they will publish your work. Many writers are excited to be accepted by an agent, only to find that two years later they still have no publisher. Also, you need to be aware that finding an agent who is willing to look at (let alone accept) your manuscript is only slightly less difficult than finding a publisher. And the agent will also likely ask you to make some significant revisions to your manuscript so that they can sell it to a publisher.

If this process sounds long and complex, it is. But it is the 'official' process as it has evolved and currently exists. But because it is so complex, many writers try to go straight to a publisher. Some publishers accept manuscripts directly from authors, and many authors choose to self-publish or go with a very small press for their first novel in order to build up their author profile. Still, if you have no better plan, you may as well consider getting on the official beaten path and see what happens.

If publication is so difficult, why bother?

Why are writers so eager to be published? Tim Winton observed in a recent ABC interview that almost everyone who sings in the shower secretly hopes someone hears them and enjoys the singing. Even writers who write, ostensibly for their own pleasure, hope that some of their writing will be read and enjoyed by others one day. And the best way for this to occur is through some form of publication.

The Spanish writer Carlos Ruiz Zafón captured this desire well in a passage from *The Angel's Game*, a part of his *Cemetery of Forgotten Books* series.

> A writer never forgets the first time they accepted a few coins or a word of praise in exchange for a story. They will never forget the sweet poison of vanity in their blood, and the belief that, if they succeed in not letting anyone discover their lack of talent, the dream of literature will provide them with a roof over their head, a hot meal at the end of the day, and what they covet the most: their name printed on a miserable piece of paper that will surely outlive them.[3]

Even if you end up only being able to publish your work online or through a small self-published print run, it is still an important achievement. You have taken the project as far as you can and others can now enjoy the work. Maybe you only end up selling a hundred copies of your book, but there is nothing like the satisfaction of encountering that first fan who tells you they have read the book twice and cannot wait for the next one. You are now free to move on to the next project, and to aim even higher both in terms of the quality of your work, and of publication success.

Exercise: Overcoming fear of publishing

Publishing anxiety is a real thing. You are far from the only writer to experience it. Sometimes, you simply have to take a bold step to overcome the fear. Identify a poem or short story you have written. Go online or use a printed guide to publishing to identify at least three possible journals or collections (either online or hard copy) where your poem or short story might be published. Look at the procedures for submission. These days, most will be done online. Provide the required information, usually short author bio, a statement that the piece has not been previously published and basic contact details, and the attachment of the poem or short story. Then take a deep breath and push the send button. Take note that nothing bad has happened to you. True, it could be that no one responds. Or if they do it is only to say that your work doesn't fit their current or upcoming issues. But at least you have broken the ice and put our work out there. And who knows, someone might say 'yes'.

3 Adapted from Carlos Ruiz Zafón, *The Angel's Game*, tr. Lucia Graves, 3.

CHAPTER 25:

Reading the Bible as a Writer

> *'There is no shortage of biblical writings ... which, if read by people of understanding – even if they are more interested in the content than in the eloquence of the language – will not fail to imbue them with something of the eloquence of the texts they are reading. This eloquence of style will only be increased if a person puts it into practice in their own writing and speaking.'*
>
> – St Augustine[1]

Good writers read. Great writers read even more. The literary tastes of great writers are as varied as their styles, yet they all seek out the best-crafted works for both their professional and leisure reading. Writers are not 'naturals'. They learn their craft. Reading great works of literature is one of the most important ways in which this occurs.

I recently read Colin Thiele's biography of the famous South Australian landscape artist Hans Heysen.[2] One thing that struck me was Heysen's interest in the great artists of the past. Whenever he travelled, he spent as much time as he could in art galleries. He didn't just look at landscape artists or those with styles similar to his own. Heysen studied and made notes about the brush technique, colours, use of light, forms and lines of artists of all styles and mediums. Why would he spend so much time studying Renaissance frescoes in Italian churches, or the works of Dutch portrait masters when he didn't do religious frescoes or portraits? Simple. Great painters learn from and are inspired by other great painters, even if they have no inclination to produce similar works. For the same reason, great fantasy writers do not read only fantasy, great romance writers do not read only romance, and great biographers do not read only biography. A writer of fantasy fiction can learn much more

1 St Augustine, *On Christian Doctrine*, trans. D.W. Robertson, book 4, iii.

2 Colin Thiele (author of *Storm Boy*, *Sun on the Stubble* and other novels) and Hans Heysen (famous landscape painter) are both South Australian icons. Colin Thiele. *Heysen of Hahndorf* (Adelaide: Rigby Limited, 1968).

from a well-crafted military history or travel book than from a poorly written fantasy novel.

Many successful writers have produced lists of their favourite works of literature, and aspiring writers often seek to read as many of the books or authors on these lists as possible. The works of Homer, the plays of Shakespeare and Shaw, the American colloquial masterpieces of Twain, Dickens' vivid depictions of the underbelly of London, the poetic beauty of Auden, the fantasy of Tolkien, all appear regularly on such lists. Yet studies of citations, references and imitations of style suggest that the most influential literary source is one that most writers do not think to add to their favourite books lists. It is the Bible. No other literary source has contributed more figures of speech, more sayings, more allusions, more frequently copied characters, than the Bible. There is a huge gap between the Bible and the next most influential source, the works of Homer – which you should also read!

So why is the Bible so influential? Is it simply the fact that so many people have read it, or that it is taken as a source of divine wisdom? These points surely play a role, but it is more than that. The various works contained in the Bible are also great literature. Robert Alter studied the Hebrew Bible hoping to add to the knowledge of biblical studies from the point of view of a literature expert. But he found something quite unexpected. He wrote: 'I also discovered for myself something unanticipated in the course of minutely examining many biblical texts: that the Bible on its part has a great deal to teach anyone interested in narrative because its seemingly simple, wonderfully complex art offers such splendid illustrations of the primary possibilities of narrative.'[3]

If you have never read a book about the Bible as literature, you might, like Alter, be surprised by what you discover. Some works to begin with are Leland Ryken's *Words of Delight! A Literary Introduction to the Bible*; Jeanie Crain's *Reading the Bible as Literature: An Introduction*; Robert Alter's *The Art of Biblical Narrative;* and Robert Alter and Frank Kermode's *The Literary Guide to the Bible.*[4]

---

3 Robert Alter, *The Art of Biblical Narrative* (New York: Harper-Collins, 1981), ix, x.

4 Ryken, *Words of Delight* (Grand Rapids: Baker, 1992); Crain, *Reading the Bible as Literature* (Cambridge: Polity, 2010); Alter, *The Art of Biblical Narrative* (New York: Basic Books, 1981); Alter and Kermode, *The Literary Guide to the Bible* (London: Fontana Press, 1989).

Even for many Christians, the literary diversity and richness of the biblical writers often comes as a surprise. When Christians read the Bible we often read a single verse, or even a few words, then stop to meditate and reflect on them. We seldom read a story or poem straight through as we would any other work of literature. We often fail to take notice of the type of literature or the human creativity involved. We are too busy looking for divine guidance. The irony is that because we overlook these features, we often miss the true message of the text. But that is a matter for a discussion of biblical hermeneutics.

I want instead to address you as writers. Specifically, I want to address you as writers with a commitment of faith in Jesus Christ. I want to challenge you to stop reading the Bible simply as a devotional book. That is not to say that you should not read the Bible as a devotional book. Of course you should. But you should also be willing to pick up the Bible and read it as a connoisseur of great literature. Be prepared to read the Bible as a writer, seeking to hone your craft. If you are not able to do this as a Christian writer, if you are not able to allow the Bible to have a literary influence upon you as it has on so many great writers of the past, then you unnecessarily impoverish yourself.

What follows are ten lessons to be learned from reading the Bible as a writer.

1. If something important is being said, then it is important to say it well. Augustine of Hippo was one of the best teachers of the art of rhetoric, or public speaking and persuasion, of his day. When he converted to Christianity in the late fourth century he allowed himself to be persuaded that the worldly craft of rhetoric had no place in the service of the gospel. After many years of listening to unnecessarily bad sermons he finally had enough. He wrote a little book titled *On Christian Doctrine* in which he included a lengthy section on the value of rhetoric for the Christian. He demonstrated that many biblical writers, especially Paul and the gospel writers, were masters of the art and used a number of complex and beautiful rhetorical devices. If the Bible can contain the best rhetorical devices, then why shouldn't Christians use them to teach and preach and write? It made no sense to Augustine that the defenders of the truth should put people to sleep with boring speaking and offend their intelligence with illogical reasoning while the proponents of

error were entertaining, making people laugh and cry, and put their arguments in the most reasonable form possible. Where was the sense in that, he asked?[5] Or, as the Christian rock musician Larry Norman famously asked in the 1970s: 'Why should the Devil have all the good music?' If the Bible can entertain, stir our emotions, and tell a gripping tale – why should we not seek to follow this example and make our writing the best it can be?

2. There is no single approved literary genre or style that the Christian writer must use. Some years ago my sons were spending time in America with their grandfather, a proudly self-proclaimed fundamentalist Christian. He berated them for having an interest in pop music, and was outraged that they also were fond of rap. They should know these were the devils' forms of music. The debate arose as they were riding with their grandfather in his car. They pointed out that he was listening to Country and Western music on the radio. To make matters worse, they had actually been paying attention to the lyrics! 'That's different,' he insisted. 'Country and Western is a form of music that is pleasing to God. Rap, rock and pop are not.' It was as simple as that. He turned the volume up on his radio and refused to engage in any further discussion.

   When a Christian writers' group I belong to put together a collection of Christian vampire stories a few years ago in an effort to reach readers we would not otherwise connect with and show that there is no place so dark that the light of the gospel cannot penetrate, we received thanks and praise from some quarters, and rabid condemnation – including death threats and even physical assault, from others.[6] There are those who are convinced that a whole range of literary genres, themes and styles are no-go zones for Christians. There are even websites dedicated to denouncing all fantasy writing, including that of C.S. Lewis, as unchristian. Such ideas, however, certainly do not come from the Bible. The Bible never teaches that certain styles of music or literature are not allowed. Instead, the Bible includes the entire range of literary types which spanned the ancient world from the Semitic cultures of the Middle East to that of the Greeks and Romans.

5 St Augustine. *On Christian Doctrine*. Book 4, chapter 2.

6 M. Worthing, ed. *Something in the Blood; Vampire Tales with a Christian Bite* (Melbourne: Morning Star Publishing, 2015).

As an exercise, before reading further, take a moment to see how many different literary genres you can name that are contained in the Bible.

Here are some you may have come up with: History (Kings, Chronicles, Samuel, Acts), philosophy (Job, Ecclesiastes), military history (Joshua and Judges), satire (Jonah), humour (Story of Ehud, Elijah's taunting of the prophets of Baal on Mt Carmel), love story (Ruth), erotic poetry (Song of Songs), alphabet poems (Psalm 119), concentric structured poetry (Isaiah 43:1-7), laments (various Psalms), wise sayings (Proverbs), letters (New Testament epistles), apocalyptic (Daniel, Revelation), drama (Job, Revelation), tragedy (Mark's Gospel), song lyrics (Psalms, the Magnificat, Philippians 2:5-11), morality stories (Nathan's speech to David, many of the Parables of Jesus), speeches (Stephen's speech, Acts 7), sermons (Paul at the Areopagus, Acts 17), prayers (John 17, Lord's prayer), genealogies (Genesis 5, Matthew 1), and biography (Matthew, Mark, Luke and John).

3. Many biblical type scenes are embedded into our Western narrative consciousness. A type scene is a recurring scene in which everyone knows what is going to happen as soon as the scene begins. Type scenes are also common in modern cinema. The car chase scene, the potential lovers who at first hate each other scene, the desperado shootout scene, etc. The scenes are either delivered to script, or deliberately altered in some way to make a point. Either way they work. Can you think of any type scenes from biblical stories? Some that come to mind are: the barren mother giving birth, the wicked king meeting a bad end, journeys into the wilderness, the hero meeting his wife at a well, the outnumbered army securing an unexpected victory, and the healing of a widow's son.[7] We can learn much about type scenes and how to use them creatively through the biblical narratives. For instance, look at the Old Testament type scenes of a man meeting his wife at a well (Jacob and Isaac), and the New Testament spin on this type scene with Jesus and the woman at the well, which takes the story in a very different direction.

7 For a good discussion of biblical type scenes, see Robert Alter, *The Art of Biblical Narrative*.

4. The gospels have given us the literary messianic figure who comes to rescue us and achieves this through supernatural powers and abilities and by sacrificing his life, achieving victory through apparent defeat. Messianic figures that bear significant and even intentional similarity to Jesus are found in everything from movie blockbusters like the *Matrix* Trilogy[8] to comic book series such as *Superman*. Even Tolkien makes use of this imagery, though he intentionally divided the messianic role in *The Lord of the Rings* between three separate characters to prevent any one of them from seeming to be a Jesus figure. (Can you guess the three and how each takes on part of the messianic role? Hint: the suffering servant who humbly puts others before his own welfare, the high priest who himself becomes a sacrifice, the coming king who inaugurates a new era of peace.) Tolkien's friend C.S. Lewis, in contrast, had no qualms about Aslan representing Jesus in a near complete allegory in his *Chronicles of Narnia* books. Writers are always interested in characters and their development. We should not overlook the fact that Jesus, as portrayed in the Gospels, is the best known and most influential literary character of all time. Understanding the story and character of Jesus as he is portrayed in the Gospels helps us to recognise the prototype for a whole host of messianic literary characters that have followed. As Christian writers we may wish to intentionally include a messianic character in our story to illustrate who Jesus was, such as C.S. Lewis did with Aslan, or Richard Bach with *Illusions: The Adventures of a Reluctant Messiah*.[9] However, we will need to know when and how to deviate our character from the standard messianic type of Jesus. Perhaps, like Tolkien, we will want to avoid any one character appearing to be messianic. But this requires a knowledge of what elements make up the Jesus messianic type.[10]
5. The Bible's great themes of sin and salvation have become the core of many works of literature. The more familiar you are with these

---

8 Mark Worthing, *The Matrix Revealed. The Theology of the Matrix Trilogy* (Adelaide: Pantaenus, 2004), 24ff.

9 Bach, *Illusions*. (New York: Bantam Doubleday Dell Publishing Group, 1994)

10 For a more detailed study of the Jesus and literary and cinematic messiah figures, see the work of Paul Armishaw, *Superman, Myth and the Narrative Apologetic*. (unpublished Ph.D. thesis, Tabor Adelaide, 2019).

biblical themes, the more richly you can explore them in your own writing. George Eliot's *Silas Marner* is a good example. Dicken's *A Christmas Carol* is another. Can you think of some others? Many great works of literature touch people deeply precisely because they explore human depravity and elements of hope and grace. A well-grounded biblical understanding of these themes which have shaped so much of our thinking helps the writer to develop them more fully and appropriately. For the Christian writer, these themes provide the opportunity to present a gospel-infused storyline without writing overtly 'religious' literature.

6. Good writing today still abounds in biblical references and allusions.[11] But you will only be able to make use of these if you know them well yourself. If you do not want to be a Judas to your craft, fail to show the wisdom of Solomon or the patience of Job in your writing, make the readers your scapegoat, or wash your hands of the whole problem of biblical allusions and wipe the dust of the issue from your shoes, choosing to be a Martha instead of a Mary, or jinx your next project, becoming a Jonah; then it may be time to gird your loins, enter the lion's den of literary critics, and bear your writer's cross by fighting the good fight of biblical literacy with some well-placed biblical allusions. Just don't overdo it.
7. The Bible contains some of the most tightly written works in all of literature. The biblical writers were masters of understatement and minimalism. If you want to use words sparingly and wisely, saying a lot in as few words as possible, there are few better places from which to learn this art than from biblical stories. It is these profound 'blink and you will miss it' comments and actions, picked up only by the attentive reader, that stand as a hallmark of good writing. Over-explanation is the curse of many writers who feel that the more words they use to tell a story, and the more obvious they make each point, the better. Examples of biblical narrative which derives its force from tight writing include the story of the tower of Babel (Genesis 11:1-10), the assassin Ehud (Judges 3:15-26), the prologue to Job (Job 1-2), Jesus' parables, and the story of Peter and John healing the lame

11 See for instance *Biblical Images in Literature*, ed. R. Bartel, J. Ackerman, and T. Warshaw (Nashville: Abingdon Press, 1975).

man (Acts 3:1-10). The Bible can be extremely succinct, leaving room for great imagination and discussion. Take, for example, the very unusual and dramatic story of Elisha and the she-bears, which comprises only two verses (2 Kings 2:23,24), or the very succinct and powerful description of Jesus's response at hearing that his friend Lazarus has died (John 11:35, KJV).

8. Reading biblical prose and poetry can provide the writer with inspiration for new styles, forms and structures. The chiastic and concentric structures found in many Hebrew poems as well as in some Hebrew prose can provide a new way of thinking about how we structure our story, novel or poem – working from the outsides (beginning and end) toward the centre, which will contain the key insight or turning point. Isaiah 43:1-7 is a powerful example of such a poem. We might also be inspired by the use of parallelism, or some of the rhetorical forms found in the New Testament epistles such as *gradatio* (ladders), *circuiti* (loops), *caesa* (pauses), rhetorical questions, chiasms, and many more.
9. Biblical literature can provide inspiration for new themes and story ideas. So much is left unsaid in the biblical accounts that the writer is almost invited to explore the situations and characters further. A classic example is Pär Lagerkvist's novel *Barabbas*,[12] in which he follows the life of Barabbas after he is set free in Jesus' place. A more recent example is that of Valerie Volk's book *Bystanders*[13] which looks at well-known biblical stories from the perspective of minor characters in the narrative. Another example is *If They Could Talk*, a collection of stories and poems seen from the perspective of various animals in the Bible.[14] These types of creative projects all arise from Christians reading the Bible as literature and having their imaginations inspired not only by what is said, but by the many secondary stories that are left untold.
10. Finally, the Bible is a book that shapes the lives of Christians. We read and study the Bible to form us spiritually, morally and theologically. As we engage with the various biblical texts we continue to grow

12 Pär Lagerkvist. *Barabbas* (Stockholm: Albert Bonniers förlag, 1950)

13 Valerie Volk, *Bystanders* (Adelaide: Wakefield Press, 2015)

14 Susan J. Bruce, ed. *If They Could Talk* (Melbourne: Morning Star Publishing, 2018).

and mature through our interaction with them. As wordsmiths we should also allow the Bible to mould us as readers and writers. The Bible should play a role in the growth of our imaginations, our understanding of arch-typical scenes, our feel for the big questions of sin and salvation, and our appreciation of good prose and poetry. But the Bible cannot shape and form us in these ways if we do not read it, and read it well.

Tips on reading the Bible as literature

1. Read from a translation other than what you use for your devotional reading.
2. Choose a translation that is based on dynamic equivalence (that is, which focuses on the best English rendering of what the text intends say) rather than either a literal translation or a paraphrase, as each of these lose much of the sense of the storyline. Today's NIV, while still suffering from the limitations of coming out of a single theological perspective and tradition, is quite good for this purpose. The NRSV is also not bad, though not as fluid in some of its prose.
3. Find a Bible that is not set out in double column format but in single column pages, just as most other literature.
4. Read some of the poetry, prayers and speeches in the more formal language of the KJV.
5. Ignore verse and chapter divisions. These were not in the original. Just because the chapter ends does not mean the story or section ends.
6. Read biblical texts as literature in the same places where you would sit down to read a good novel. If you read a good book on your lounge or the hammock in the backyard, do this also when you read the Bible as literature.
7. Read an entire poem, story or section of a story in one sitting without stopping to look up key words or check commentaries – just as you would read a good novel or book of poetry.
8. If you read novels with pencil in hand, marking key lines or making the occasional note in the margins, then do this also when reading the Bible as literature.
9. Recognise that the Holy Spirit inspired human beings to write, using

their own vocabularies and literary abilities as well as the literary genres known to them within their own cultural contexts.

10. If you are interested in poetry, try reading all of the poems of the Bible. Similarly, read all the short stories as a group, then perhaps all the military accounts, the histories, the letters, etc.
11. Accept that a recognition of the Bible as good literature does not diminish its status as given by divine inspiration.
12. Learn to view the Bible not as a single book just because it is bound together, but as at least sixty-six different books, including collections of poems. Remember that each individual piece of writing can stand alone as a literary work.
13. Try to read a poem or story as if you are coming to it for the first time, without strong presuppositions as to what the story is supposed to be about. For instance, do not read the Song of Songs with the long-held idea that its erotic imagery is really nothing more than a metaphor about the relationship between Christ and the church. And don't read the satirical novella Jonah with the idea that its main purpose is to demonstrate, as some sort of test of our faith, that a prophet can be swallowed by a giant fish and survive. This is a narrative device. It is not the point of the story.
14. Understand how highly God values the power of the written word. The sacred life of words is nowhere so richly experienced as in the literature of the Bible.

Exercise: Bringing the Bible to your reading group

If you belong to a reading group or book club, try this. If you do not belong to one, perhaps create an ad hoc group for the purpose. Suggest that a biblical short story such a Ruth or Jonah (or Esther or Job if a longer story is desired) be read and discussed by the group as literature. Everyone is asked to avoid saying things like 'What God said to me in this story …' and the like. Simply talk about the characters, which ones you identified with, the plot, the impact, etc. like you would any other short story. Notice how you have seen things in the story you had not seen before. Notice the new found respect you have gained for the story as literature.

CHAPTER 26:

Faith-Life Writing

> *'Anyone can write impersonally about the many facets of the Christian life. The person who wishes to inspire, to comfort, to challenge, or to heal, however, becomes personally involved with people. ... Not everyone can write this type of material. Here, more than anywhere, communication involves sharing what you yourself have experienced.'*
>
> – Margaret Anderson[1]

The story that most Christians want and need most to tell is the story of how God has worked in their own lives. Perhaps it is the story of how we came to faith in Christ. Perhaps it is the story of an answered prayer. Perhaps it is the story of finding God's love in the little things in life. But for all the importance of these stories to us and to others, we often do not tell them well. Too often we try to imitate the style of someone else's story. We want to present a 'testimony' in the style of the mid-twentieth-century revival meetings. Our stories end up sounding contrived and do not have the impact we had hoped. But they are stories we must tell. If we do not tell our stories, our expression of faith will be impersonal, formulaic, and ultimately unconvincing. The novelist Tim Winton put it well when he said, 'I learnt how perilously faith depends upon story, for without narrative there is only theological assertion, which is, in effect, inert cargo.'[2] So how do we turn the inert cargo of our assertions into compelling, living stories?

For some years now I have worked with the *Stories of Life* writing competition, which is aimed at encouraging Christians to tell their stories

1 Margaret Anderson, *The Christian Writer's Handbook*, 60.

2 Tim Winton, *The Boy behind the Curtain*, (Sydney: Random House Australia, 2016), 106.

of faith.[3] There are some amazing and encouraging stories out there, and the aim of the competition is not only to encourage people to tell their stories, but to help them to tell these stories well.

As soon as most of us begin to talk about how our faith in God has impacted our lives, a switch flicks in our brains and we begin to write in language filled with religious jargon and terms we would seldom use in everyday conversation. We end up telling the most interesting story in the most sedate or inaccessible terms. And we are convinced each story must have an unequivocally happy ending, or make some obvious and profound theological point.

In the hundreds of submissions that come in to the *Stories of Life* competition each year, we see many writers making some basic mistakes of storytelling and writing. So how do we avoid this? The following are some tips that I developed and posted on the competition's website to help writers telling a story about an experience of God in their life.

1. *Tell just one story!* If you do not stick to one main storyline or incident your short story or account will lose focus. Many writers cannot resist including aspects of their life story that are not directly related to the main narrative line. Do not introduce characters, events or facts that do not contribute to the main storyline. You might need to tell us that Uncle Cecil was the one who showed up with the dog you were given for your 10th birthday, but you do not need to tell us that he had cancer, is no longer married to your aunt, or used to play football, etc. unless these things are important to the main story.

   Remedy: Identify the main story you are telling and ask yourself whether each incident, person or bit of information you include is vital to that story.

2. *Know when to stop!* A common mistake is to add a paragraph or two of obvious explanation (often very spiritual) after what would

3 The four books that have come out of this competition so far are *A Chicken Can Make a Difference and Other Stories of Life*, ed. M. Worthing and James Cooper (Melbourne: Morning Star, 2016); *The Gecko Renewal and Other Stories of Life*, ed. J. Cooper and M. Worthing (Melbourne: Morning Star 2017); *Three Dummies in a Dinghy and Other Stories of Life*, ed. Claire Bell, J. Cooper and M. Worthing (Melbourne: Morning Star, 2018); and *Papa's Shoes and Other Stories of Life*, ed. M. Worthing, Pete Court and Claire Bell (Adelaide: Immortalise, 2019).

have been a very good and powerful natural ending. Know when your story has finished. Readers like to work out the main point or lesson for themselves. If the story is well-written, this will not be a problem. If you need to add a paragraph or two to explain that the point of the story is that God is faithful and never forgets us, then you have probably not written the story well enough and need to revisit your main story, rather than add an explanation at the end.

Remedy: Stop your story at the end and let the reader work out the obvious lesson to be learned from it. If you have shown the reader what happened, you do not need to also tell them what it means.

3. *Don't try too hard!* Overwriting can be the death of a good story. Beware of excessive use of adjectives and adverbs, as well as descriptive phrases and sentences where these do not contribute to the story or the setting. Aim for concision of language. Ask yourself what each word and phrase is doing in the story. If the answer is 'nothing', take it out. Especially when writing about God and faith, people tend to overuse adjectives and adverbs, feeling that this shows the intensity of their faith. But too much of this can simply end up detracting from the power of the story being told.

   Remedy: Edit heavily. Ask of each word what it is doing in the sentence. Keep in mind that the quality of your story can be judged by the quality of your scrap heap. Do not be afraid to throw out a favourite line or phrase if it is not doing anything in the story. And remember, God will not be upset if you delete a few excessive adjectives you have used to describe his absolutely, astounding, amazing, unfathomable, unbelievable, underserved, awesome, entirely gracious and unearned goodness.

4. *Be Christian, not religious!* Avoid excessive use of religious jargon. Some people write about coming to faith using terms and phrases that would have been incomprehensible to them at the time of the encounter they are describing. Others tend to use terms and phrases that are clearly common in their own church or tradition, but which many other Christians would find unclear or confusing. Some of this may be unavoidable, depending on your story, but when there is too much of it, it becomes a distraction. Write so that the ordinary

person will know what you are talking about. Don't tell them you were 'saved' or 'filled by the Spirit' or 'experienced the healing power of Jesus' or experienced 'eucharistic rapture'. Simply describe what happened to you using language that anyone can understand. This will make your story more readable and more effective. *Remedy*: Look at what you have written and the language used and ask: Would my non-religious family and friends understand these words and phrases?

5. *Proofreading is next to godliness!* No matter how good you think you were at English grammar in school, you need to have one or two good readers (at a minimum) read your story and suggest corrections. Obvious typos, spelling mistakes, incorrect punctuation and the like will detract from an otherwise compelling story.

   Remedy: Don't send your story off until you have had it carefully proofread. Let your friends spot your typos and misspellings, not your readers.

The following story appeared in *A Chicken Can Make a Difference.*[4] It is not the spectacular tale of my conversion from a life of crime and violence. That story would be a work of fiction. Instead, it is the simple story of a small boy trying to find a way to avoid going outdoors for recess in the dead of winter, with unexpected consequences. Our stories about our experience of God do not need to be outwardly exciting in the details. The power of the story is in its telling, and in genuine accounts of God working in the lives of ordinary people

Twice Saved

Churches were places we drove past on the way to town. They were as large as barns but usually painted white instead of red. I'd never actually been inside of one, nor do I recall any particular curiosity about what took place within them. They were simply there. My parents were married in a church, but that was the last time they had been. Christian America may have been all-pervasive, but in my early childhood it was only background scenery.

4 Edited James Cooper and Mark Worthing. (Melbourne: Morning Star, 2016), 114ff.

The only reason I heard the Gospel at all as a child was because I lived in a region that was very cold – in a part of Michigan where we had an abundance of snow, wind and ice. In winter the local churches sponsored a Bible club at my primary school that met in a small transportable parked at the end of the playground. In those days children were required to stay outside during lunch so the teachers could recover from the morning session and brace themselves for the afternoon. But if you wanted to hear Bible stories, every Wednesday you were allowed to go into this special, heated transportable for half an hour, before being sent out again to endure the last ten minutes of lunch in the biting cold. I didn't like the cold. Snowmen, snowball fights, sledding, beautiful landscapes blanketed in snow. I hated it. When you're six years old and your feet are nearly frozen through because your parents can't afford proper boots, all you care about is surviving recess so you can get back in out of the cold, the wind and the snow. So every Wednesday I went inside to hear Bible stories. After the Bible stories were over we still had to go outside into the cold for another ten minutes. But the Bible story lady always asked if there was anyone who wanted to stay and have a prayer with her.

I was in Year One and wasn't entirely sure what a prayer was, but it didn't take me long to realise that those who stayed after to have a prayer with the Bible story lady didn't have to go back outside in the cold. So after about four weeks of this routine, when she asked who would like to remain after, I raised my hand. She sat two or three of us down at a little wooden table at the back of the room and explained to us in very simple terms that Jesus – who I noticed figured in a lot of the stories – had died for our sins, which were all the bad things we did. It seemed like a pretty severe punishment for getting angry with my sister and not doing my chores on time, but I was glad it was him instead of me.

'Do you agree with that?' the Bible story lady asked, looking carefully to each one of us in turn. The correct answer that would keep me in from the cold was all too obvious. She continued, 'And Jesus did this for you because Jesus is God (that was a shocker – I was getting my characters all confused now) – and God loves you.'

It sounded good to me that God loved me, and I agreed with that as well, and not just because I was cold. Then, with great solemnity she said; 'Repeat this prayer after me.' And she said a little prayer that went basically like this; 'Dear God, I know I'm a sinner. I ask you to forgive my sins, and I put my trust in Jesus as my Saviour. Amen.' When you're six years old you tend to do what adults tell you to do, so I said the prayer. Then with a beaming smile the Bible story lady proclaimed us all Christians and saved, and recorded our names on a little notebook she had lying on the table.

Well, this all struck me as very interesting. I'd never been saved before. So I went home and told my mother and asked her what it meant – and hoped that I'd done nothing I would get in trouble for. My mother, as it turned out, had attended a little country Methodist Sunday School as a girl and was able to explain to me that I'd put my trust in God. Because of this I was a Christian and when I died I would go to heaven. This whole thing was turning out to be a lot more important than I had thought. But then I began to think, 'Does it count if I didn't know what I was saying?' I only stayed after because I was cold and I didn't want to go back outside. So I thought to myself, 'This is serious business. I'd better not stuff it up.' I waited seven very long and anxious days for Wednesday to come round again.

The next week I went again to the Bible club, and again I stayed after. The Bible story lady looked at me a long moment, then declared, 'I remember you. You stayed after last week and got saved.'

And I said, 'Yes, I'd like to say the prayer again, please.'

'Oh, you can't say it twice,' she said. 'It only counts once.'

'But,' I protested, 'last time I didn't mean it because I didn't know what I was talking about.'

She was steadfast. 'No, you can't say it again.'

I was only six, but I felt I had a lot more riding on this than she did, so I held my ground, as only a six year old can. 'I have to say it again,' I demanded. 'I won't leave until I say the prayer again.'

By now we were running short on time and the Bible story lady was clearly becoming flustered as to what to do with me. Of course, I could've just said the thing on my own anytime during the last week. But as far as I knew, this was the holy place and the appointed time. If one wanted to be saved, this was where and when it had to be. I knew I had to go back to this place and say the prayer again, this time in full knowledge of what it meant. Finally she relented and let me say the prayer with the others, but she told me she was not going to write my name down in her notebook again. After we finished and she had written down the names of the other children she looked at me sternly and warned: 'You can come back to Bible club next week, but you are not allowed to stay after. Twice is enough for anyone to be saved.'

I promised I would not stay after again. That was the last time I was saved. It would have to be enough.

Exercise: Conversion story

Write down the story of why you are a Christian. If you have grown up in a Christian family and cannot recall ever not having faith in God, then write the story of why you have remained a Christian. Tell the story in an interesting manner. What characters are involved? What were you feeling? Is there an unexpected twist or component to the story that can be left to the end? Remember, the drama can be internal as well as external. You may not have a story like Saul of Tarsus, but that does not mean you do not have a story.

CHAPTER 27:

The Importance of Writers' Groups

> *'If you are critiquing another's work ... be kind with humility. Never use critiquing as an opportunity to show how much you know. ...*
> *If your work is being critiqued ... be careful of defensiveness. It keeps us from the truth about ourselves and perpetuates self-doubt.'*
>
> – Rosanne Hawke[1]

Films often portray the solitary writer going off to some remote location to work for months or years in isolation on their masterpiece. This might be great material for movies, but in most cases, it is far from realistic. Not all writers are gregarious. Some are decidedly shy. But most have a close network of confidants who assist them with their craft in many ways.

Many consider J.R.R. Tolkien and C.S. Lewis to be among the best writers of the mid-twentieth century. Yet neither wrote in isolation. They formed a writing group with several others which they called the Inklings. It was one of the most famous and productive writing groups ever to have been formed. It was here that Tolkien, Lewis and others tried out their ideas on one another, read portions of their latest works, and heard honest comments about what did and did not work.

The story of *Literati*

In late 2004 a small group of writers connected with Tabor College in Adelaide decided to meet once a month for mutual encouragement. At the time I was a senior lecturer at the college and head of the new faculty of humanities. This meant I had a key and access to a meeting room, thus empowering me to appoint myself inaugural 'co-ordinator' of the group. So don't be timid about taking the lead in beginning a writers' group. Possessing the key to a free meeting space is more than

1 Rosanne Hawke, *Riding the Wind. Writing for Children and Young Adults*. (Melbourne: Morning Star, 2019), 36f.

sufficient qualification! The make-up of the group changed somewhat over the years as new members joined and others moved away or simply moved on. But fifteen years later the group still meets regularly, with about two-thirds of participants having been a part of the group for ten years or longer. The initial premise of the group was simple. We would meet together for pizza and coke, share our writing, and pray for each other (both writing and personal needs). After some years, with many of us growing older and becoming more conscious of health, the pizza and coke were dropped in favour of 'bring your own healthy meal'.

We generally meet for just over two hours on a Thursday night, including an initial time of informal discussion and eating. Afterward we share writing news. In the early years there wasn't too much to share, but in more recent years there have been several writing awards, book launches, acceptances of manuscripts, appearances of works in anthologies, reviews of books and the like to mention before we get started. Every second meeting we try to look at someone's manuscript in depth, and by mutual agreement we are polite – but honest. We find that it is best for a writer to participate in a few of these reviews before submitting their own manuscript for scrutiny. Occasionally we look at two manuscripts in a session if two writers have only the first half written and want feedback before going further, or if the works are short (such as novellas or YA novels). It is not only the authors presenting manuscripts that benefit from these reviews. I find that I learn a great deal from these sessions that I can apply to my own writing.

On the alternate months we have a writing challenge. These are very popular as everyone has a chance to write a small piece and receive feedback. The secret to a good writing group is providing plenty of opportunity to write and share writing. This is, after all, what writers love to do. The variety of challenges helps us sharpen our skills by focusing on writing tasks we might not otherwise undertake. We found that it is best to set a word limit on these, often 500 to 1000 words, depending on the number of participants we expect to contribute. Occasionally a challenge requires something more substantial, and we will spread the reading of them out over two sessions. While most of the writing challenges involve prose fiction, poetry and non-fiction also feature occasionally.

Exercises for writing groups

Some of the more popular exercises we have used over the years include:

- Write the first chapter of a novel in _______ genre. Sometimes we all do the same genre (e.g., sci-fi), other times we draw genres out of a hat (no trades allowed!). A few of these first chapters have been so intriguing and well-received that they went on to become actual novels.
- As a variation on the above, we provide the opening sentence from a well-known novel and each writer has to produce the next thousand words. It is surprising, for instance, where one can go with a sentence like 'In a hole in the ground there lived a hobbit.'
- Write an alternate ending for a novel that is familiar to most of the group.
- Write a story based upon an unusual photo sent around to the group that explains what is going on in the photograph.
- Write a sestina celebrating Christmas or Easter.
- Write a stream of consciousness poem with only minor edits allowed for sharing with the group.
- Write a series of six-word stories in various genres. (A variation is twitter stories of 140 characters, recently increased to 280).
- Write a short story in mixed genre (often chosen at random) such as fantasy and cooking, horror and travel, steam punk and romance, historical fiction and fantasy, etc.
- Select a classic short poem. Write a story in which each successive sentence in the story begins with the successive words of the poem. When done correctly, the poem can be reconstructed simply by reading the first word of each sentence. This is harder than is sounds and forces everyone to think very carefully about how to end each sentence and how to get from point A to B in the narrative. The best stories are the ones that do not sound at all constrained by the requirement of pre-chosen first words of sentences.
- If a group member has recently had a novel published, challenge everyone to write a humorous deleted scene from that novel.
- Recording dialogue. Have two group members with some acting

ability (or pretentions thereto!) act out a small scene from a play, or simply something they have made up. Afterwards give everyone fifteen minutes to write down as dialogue what they have just seen.

- Remember those school writing projects to start each new academic year? Please write about what you did over your summer holidays. Try it now. As a variation, we suggested that people could choose to write either about something that really happened to them over the break, or they could make something up. The rest of the group is tasked with deciding whether they have just heard a piece of fiction or non-fiction.
- Write a novella of less than 20 000 words. Two to three of these can be looked at in successive meetings until everyone has had a turn. This is a good project for a long-running group that wants a bigger challenge and is happy to take a break from smaller exercises.
- Write a story or poem from the perspective of one of the animals of the Bible.
- Write a detective story of less than 1500 words in which all the characters are based upon other members of the writers' group. Choose carefully who you decide to kill off!
- If a group member has recently had a major publication, challenge everyone to write a review. The best reviews should be posted on the author's and reviewer's websites or blogs afterward.
- Write an occasional poem. This is not a poem that is written occasionally, but a poem written to mark or commemorate a particular occasion. Chose an event that everyone in the group will be aware of (either good or bad) on the world stage, or perhaps an event of more local interest, like the wedding of one of the group's members.
- If a picture can paint a thousand words, then a thousand words should be able to describe a picture, right? Distribute an image of a painting, or perhaps a few to choose from, and challenge everyone to describe the images in that painting in 1000 words. This is a great exercise for descriptive writing.

Work on a group project

Some good group projects for your local writers' group might include:

- Putting on a mini book day or writers' fair,
- Producing a collection of poems on a certain theme.
- Producing an anthology of short stories.
- Organising a writing competition for local schools.
- Bringing a guest writer/speaker to your town.
- Organising a 'meet the writer(s)' day at your local library.
- Organising a writing retreat for the group.

My own writers' group has produced two anthologies in recent years, one a collection of Christian Vampire stories, and the other (much safer!), a collection of Bible stories written from the perspective of the animals. Such works are good fun and a great chance to work together while gaining editing, publishing and marketing skills. There is no shame in self-publishing such works as a group and selling them to family and friends. And who knows, you might even find a proper publisher for your collection.

Different types of writing groups

Not every group will suit the needs of each writer. Some groups are more formal than others. Some focus on giving advice and tips, others simply on encouragement. There are groups just for women, for new writers, for Christians, for writers of a particular genre, for poets and for published writers. Groups vary in size from three (two is not a group!) to up to a dozen or more. In my own experience, once the group size hits fifteen to twenty it becomes unwieldy and probably needs to split into two groups. Most groups meet in person, but there are also online groups. Ask around and check with local writers' support groups to see what is in your area and suits you. If you cannot find anything, consider seeking out one or two like-minded writers and starting your own group.

Whatever kind of writer you are, working in isolation is an occupational hazard, and should be avoided. You need encouragement, feedback, tips on proofreaders and publishers, etc. The best way to achieve this on a regular basis is to become part of a writing group. Think of it as a writers' cooperative. You might feel guilty asking the same friends over and over to read your latest chapters and comment on your story, or to help you with proofreading, or to help set up for your book launch. But if you are regularly performing these tasks for others, you will not feel you are putting them out when you ask for their help in turn.

Writers' conferences

Not everyone will be able to easily find a writers' group that works for them. Time, distance, and differing agendas all play a role. Another way to begin networking with other writers is to attend a writers' conference. Increasingly, there are a number of specifically Christian writers' conferences on offer. These are held regularly in most regions of the US. In Australia, Omega Writers holds a major conference each year.[2] There are also a number of smaller one-off conferences and workshops that you can find through a careful search of the net, or by simply asking around. Also, check with the local Writers' Centre in your state, territory or region to see what's on offer.

The writers' conference provides a good chance to get away for the week or weekend, bring your laptop or notebook, and do some writing. It is an opportunity to connect with other writers, hear some encouraging speakers, buy some books, and meet some editors and publishers. For the Christian writer, attending a dedicated Christian writers' conference also provides an opportunity to connect with like-minded people to discuss the unique challenges of writing for a Christian market, of Christian publishing, and of dealing responsibly with faith issues in your writing. I know many writers who have come back from such conferences unable to stop talking about all they learned. Others had wished there was more focus on their own preferred genre, but I can recall no one who has regretted going, or who has not immediately begun to make plans to attend the next conference.

2 Find Omega Writers at www.omegawriters.org

CHAPTER 28:

The Writer's Personal Library

> *'I don't read in order to study the craft; I read because I like to read. ... I don't read fiction to study the art of fiction, but simply because I like stories. Yet there is a learning process going on. Every book you pick up has its own lesson or lessons, and quite often the bad books have more to teach than the good ones.'*
>
> – Stephen King[1]

One of the richest descriptions of the influence of a life surrounded by books comes from C.S. Lewis. On the importance of books in his home as a child Lewis wrote:

> My father bought all the books he read and never got rid of any of them. There were books in the study, books in the drawing room, books in the cloakroom, books (two deep) in the great bookcase on the landing, books in a bedroom, books piled as high as my shoulder in the cistern attic, books of all kinds reflecting every transient stage of my parents' interest, books readable and unreadable, books suitable for a child and books most emphatically not. Nothing was forbidden me. In the seemingly endless rainy afternoons I took volume after volume from the shelves. I had always the same certainty of finding a book that was new to me as a man who walks into a field has of finding a new blade of grass.[2]

C.S. Lewis was certainly fortunate as a budding writer in his choice of parents! We do not all have such a richness of literature at our early disposal. I had a King James Bible, a battered *Webster's Dictionary*, a copy of *Grimm's Fairy Tales*, and an 1898 set of *Encyclopaedia Britannica* passed down by my great grandparents. But I made full use of what I had. If the space to explore was limited, then I explored it all the more thoroughly. As soon as I was old enough to begin to find and buy my own books, I began a collection that has not stopped growing since.

1 Stephen King, *On Writing. A Memoir of the Craft*, 164.

2 Cited in Corey Latta, *C.S. Lewis and the Art of Writing* (Eugene, OR: Cascade Books, 2016), 14.

If someone takes up an apprenticeship as an automotive mechanic, they soon find they need to acquire a number of tools which allow them to do their job and do it well. A good chef will spend several thousand dollars on a quality set of knives, and a keen athlete will have a room full of specialised training gear, shoes, outfits and other items vital to pursuing their sport. For the writer, such items as pen, notebook and computer are clearly essential. But a good writer needs more than just the materials for putting words onto paper, or to save them onto a computer file. A good writer needs books.

Books on the art of writing

There are hundreds of books in print about writing. In fact, you are reading one of them now.[3] Having a few good books on writing will be helpful if you need to look something up, get stuck with core issues like plot, character, openings and the like, or if you just want to go over some basic advice again for inspiration or as a refresher. A number of successful authors have written books on writing that are as much autobiography as an introduction to the art of writing. These are not often as informative as textbooks on writing, but they are almost always inspiring.

Books on publishing

At some point you will need to begin submitting your poems, short stories and novels. There are a range of books about publishing, and you should have a few recent ones on hand to make sure that when the time comes, you present your work in the best possible way, and to the right places. There are also books that list publishers, literary agents, writing assessment groups and writing competitions.[4] Having an up-to-date book that lists these contacts is essential when the time comes to submit your work.

---

3 A complete list of good books on writing would be impossibly long. But I would like to point to the recently published work by my former lecturing colleague at Tabor Adelaide, Rosanne Hawke. Her book, *Riding the Wind: Writing for Children and Young Adults* (Melbourne: Morning Star Publishing, 2019) is a very readable and practical resource to start with not just for children's and YA authors, but for any writer seeking to hone their craft.
4 Cf. for instance the most recent editions of *The Australian Writer's Marketplace* (Brisbane: Queensland Writers Centre) and *The Christian Writers Market Guide* (Steve Laube, Nashville: The Christian Writers Institute).

Genre books

If you are a writer of fantasy, you will want a good fantasy library. You may want to be careful reading other fantasy while you are in the midst of one of your own novels, as some find that they begin to unintentionally imitate the style of what they are reading, but you will want to be well read in your general field. You need to know what the classics are in your genre, as well as what the current trends are and what authors are currently in vogue. You do not need to imitate these writers, but you should be reasonably abreast of what they are doing. It is like fine-dining chefs. The good ones go out to eat at other good restaurants in their free time so they can see what other chefs are doing, and leave inspired with new ideas of their own.

Books outside your preferred genre

Never read only within your own preferred genre. If you are a committed historical fiction writer, you need to push yourself to read widely from genres other than historical fiction. This helps keep your own writing fresh. And you might be surprised where new ideas can come from. Some types of reading suggest themselves naturally. If you write fantasy with big battle scenes, military history will be of great benefit. If you write sci-fi, you will want to read plenty of popular science, if you write works that are heavily character-based, then biographies and autobiographies will be of benefit. If people say your prose is too heavy or cumbersome, try adding some YA novels to your reading list.

Classics

A good writer's library will have a solid collection of classic literature that is not only on display, but also read. This includes the classics from Greek dramas and Roman histories, to milestone works like *Beowulf* and the *Canterbury Tales*, to more recent classics. Even if you do not write in these genres and styles, you can always learn from the masters. Some writers (and keen readers) like to read all the books that win a certain award, or are shortlisted, in order to see what is being judged as the best in current literature. In this way they end up reading books they might not otherwise look at. I know of several people, for instance, who read every book shortlisted for the annual Man Booker prize.

Poetry

Most writers want to produce novels. But having a good collection of poetry will help you appreciate the beauty of language. When you read poetry you gain a renewed sense of how important each word choice is, of the sound of words, of the precision of language. At least a few decent books of poetry, in a range of styles, should grace the shelves of any good fiction writer. And if you are a writer of poetry, your collection should be extensive, for good poems are works as much to be studied as to be enjoyed.

General resource books

In my library I keep a couple of shelves of resource books close to my writing desk. I find myself turning to them again and again. The books you should have include:

- Dictionaries. Have one or two trusted, easy to reference, single-volume dictionaries nearby. Only buy hardcover, as soft cover dictionaries will not stand up to frequent use. While a bit unwieldy, consider also investing in the Oxford English two-volume dictionary for those situations in which you are looking for something a bit more than just the basics. If you write for and publish in more than one English-speaking context, as is today often the case, then have a good dictionary from each context. For instance a British and American dictionary used together can reveal not only some of the more obvious and easy to manage spelling differences, but also some of the more subtle nuances of meaning between the two major forms of the language used today.
- Grammars. At least one good grammar is vital. You may have thought (or hoped) you had seen the last of such books when you finished high school, but a good grammar book can get you out of a tight spot. If you have a sentence structure that just doesn't quite work, a good grammar (if you have learned how to use it) can probably explain to you why. If you struggle with clearly written language, perhaps just read a chapter from time to time at random to see what you can pick up.
- Books on punctuation. While this is often included within the broader context of grammar, there are a number of books specialising in

punctuation. My experience as an editor has convinced me that even good writers struggle with knowing when to use a comma, when to use a colon instead of a semi-colon, how to punctuate dialogue, and when and how to use dashes as punctuation marks. One of the best-written and most popular books available on punctuation is *Eats, Shoots and Leaves: The Zero Tolerance Approach to Punctuation* by Lynne Truss (2003). There are other books out there, but they are not nearly as entertaining.

- Thesauruses. A variety of these exist, and you may want two or three to make sure you have covered all the possibilities. While essential for poets, many prose writers would benefit from stopping more often to consult a thesaurus to see if there are other words that could be used to get their meaning across.
- Rhyming dictionaries. This is a tool that is mostly for poets. But even if you do not write rhymed verse, it can be a useful thing to have around – just in case!
- Foreign language dictionaries. Many writers like to add a few foreign words to their work sometimes, especially if they have a foreign character, or their writing is set in another time or place. If this is your habit, a few good dictionaries representing the language you are either familiar with, or likely to want to use, will do you a world of good. They are also handy when reading authors who like to use the occasional foreign word or phrase. I find that Latin, French, German, Italian and Spanish dictionaries are the ones that are most handy for English language readers and writers.
- Strunk and White. This book, titled *The Elements of Style*, was first published in 1919 by William Strunk and revised in 1959 by E.B. White. It is a style guide, but for all intents and purposes, is in a category of one. You must not only own a copy but have read it. It is about writing clearly and concisely. Whether you write speeches, academic works or romance novels, the guidelines and advice in this book are a must. Its short, concise sections cover almost every conceivable habit of bad writing, and give easy to understand instructions on how to correct them.

The Christian writer will also want to have:

- Bibles. As a Christian you will of course want a few good Bibles. But as a writer you need to be attentive to the nuances of biblical stories and the different ways they might be translated. You may also find that you sometimes need to quote from the Bible and you will want to have some good options ready at hand. The King James is a classic and its influence on English literature in immense. It is dated and seldom used in contemporary Christian worship or devotion these days, but you should definitely have a copy. Add to this a variety of newer translations ranging from very readable (Good News) to the accurate and respectable (NRSV) and a range of options in between.
- Bible commentaries. It will cost quite a bit to get quality commentaries on the whole Bible, so perhaps an affordable set that covers everything generally, and more expensive works for biblical books you are likely to study or consult more often. If you are writing biblical fiction, quality commentaries covering the texts that form the foundation and background to your narrative will be essential.
- A Bible concordance. If you are trying to find a verse you remember is in the Bible somewhere, or wonder in what contexts a certain word might be used, or want to find out what the original Hebrew or Greek for that word is, then a quality concordance can help you do all these things. It's sort of like a street directory to the Bible (the old hard copy kind, not the GPS kind!)
- A Bible dictionary. Use of a Bible Dictionary is a quick way to check key words, themes, persons and places in the Bible to make sure your allusion or reference fits.
- A good book on the Bible as literature. Leland Ryken's *Words of Delight. A Literary Introduction to the Bible* (Grand Rapids, Baker) is something of a classic and is a good start. Robert Alter's *The Art of Biblical Narrative* and *The Art of Biblical Poetry* (both by Basic Books, New York) are great for the Hebrew Bible
- A good book on the influence of the Bible on literature.[5] The Bible

---

5 One good example of such texts that I have found useful, though now a bit dated, is *Biblical Images in Literature*, ed. R. Bartel, J. Ackerman and T. Warshaw (Nashville: Abingdon Press, 1975).

has provided more sayings and images to English Literature than any other single source. Familiarity with how and where this has occurred in the past may provide inspiration for how to use biblical expressions and images in your own writing.

- Works of significant Christian writers in your field of writing. If you want to write mainstream novels, but as a Christian, find other Christian writers who have written for the mainstream and see how their faith impacted their own writing. If you want to write Christian romance or Christian fantasy, then find some good contemporary examples of these to read and include them in your library.
- A general church history. The history of the church is filled with fascinating characters and events that you may want to make reference to. A good church history book, with an extensive index, is the best way to get the names, dates and locations right.
- A summary of Christian belief. If you at all intend to bring specific Christian themes and ideas into your writing, why not take the time to get these right. If your story is ultimately about sin and redemption, having a good idea of what these concepts entail will help you to bring them out in your writing.
- Some books on Christianity and the arts. If you are not only writing as a Christian, but writing Christian-themed works, then you are participating in the very long, rich and sometimes complex history of Christianity and the arts. It would be good to know a bit of the context in which you are working.
- A few books of art works based on biblical stories and themes. These can be a rich source of inspiration to the writer seeking to describe a scene in words that visual artists have previously sought to portray in images.

Finally, your library should include at least four copies of everything you have published, whether an article, a poem, a short story or an entire book. The first copy is your working copy for making notes and corrections in case the work is ever revisited, the second is to set on a shelf and display for posterity, the third is to lend out, and the fourth is to replace the third copy when it doesn't come back! If you are able to buy copies of your books at wholesale cost (and most authors can do this) then consider having a few copies on hand to sell to that person you inevitably meet who says, 'I'd love to buy a copy of your book, but I'm not sure where I can find one.'

Buying all of these books in one hit will cost a small fortune, and you may have difficulty finding the best ones for your needs in a short time. Build your personal library book by book. Keep an eye out for second-hand books and discount books which will fill holes in your library without costing too much. As the books come in, get to know them so that you know what you have and can readily turn to them when needed. Not every book is meant to be read cover to cover, but you should be familiar with what lies between the covers of each of your books, and what use you might make of it in future.

Exercise: Starting your writer's library

Grab an eco-friendly, re-usable cloth shopping bag from your pantry. Go to your local bookstore. If you are on a tight budget (and of course you are, you are a writer, after all) then go to your local second-hand bookshop. Fill the bag with books that will be helpful for you as a writer. Reference works like specialised dictionaries and thesauruses, books on writing, books of poetry, collections of short stories by well-known writers, baby name books, books similar to what you would like to write … anything you think you might use. Pay for the books! Take them home and find or build a shelf for them. Congratulations. You have now started your writer's resource library. Repeat the process as often as time and funds allow.

CHAPTER 29:

The Future of Books and Writers

> *'Though ebooks were slated to overtake print books by 2015, that just hasn't happened. There are a few simple reasons for this: print books are theft resistant, they don't run out of power, and you can easily pass them on when you are done.'*
>
> – Sheeraz Raza[1]

The business of writers is books. It is important, therefore, that writers understand the various aspects of the world of books. The death of publishing, and of books themselves, has been predicted for so long that it has become tiresome. For decades now new libraries have been designed far too small, by planners assuming the rise of the internet or the imminent arrival of e-books will spell the end of the book as we know it. In my career as an academic I have been part of more than one library review in which some expert or another assured an institution that they would need far less library space in future since all the important resources would be online. Of course, many important resources have been put online, and some academic resources are no longer available in hard copy. However, books have continued to proliferate, and those institutions who bought into the view that they would need less library space in future soon found themselves struggling for space within their new facilities.

Similarly, early in the present century the demise of the traditional book (and bookstore) through e-books was confidently predicted – then repeatedly postponed. Now, few talk about e-books replacing print books any time soon.

This, of course, is not to say that nothing is changing in the world of books. But these changes have not been as rapid and revolutionary as has often been predicted. Yet great changes are occurring, and have long been occurring, in the world of books.

1 Sheeraz Raza, 'EBooks Vs Physical Copies', Value Walk, 23 June 2016. https://www.valuewalk.com/2016/06/ebooks-vs-physical-copies-infographic. Accessed 24.01.2019.

From scroll to codex

Books began as soon as writing began. The only reason to write something is to preserve it. The earliest writings were on clay tablets (the cuneiform of early Mesopotamia). Whole libraries of these tablets have been found. At the time, those who transcribed and stored them must have been convinced that their system would never be surpassed. Yet the tablets were heavy, hard to store, and broke if dropped. The discovery that papyrus could be used to write on was revolutionary.

Then, instead of stacking pieces of papyrus on top of one another, someone discovered that they could be connected in a long row, then rolled up, often with wooden dowels at each end to assist with the process. Thus the scroll was born. The great library of Alexandria, which contained tens of thousands of books, consisted of pigeon holes into which scrolls of various sizes were inserted. These were read by being unrolled in one direction while being simultaneously rolled up in the other, allowing the reader to follow the progression of the text. Scribes meticulously made new copies from existing scrolls. Those scribes and learned people who worked with them must have believed that there could never be a more efficient form of the book than the scroll.

Yet a few centuries after Christ, with the sturdier vellum (thin, pressed calf leather) and other forms of animal-based parchment in use for writing, someone found that pages could be bound together, forming what we might consider the first modern book. It was efficient for finding the right place in the text without unrolling an entire scroll, and it was easy to lay an existing book open beside unbound, blank pages in order to make new copies. It was a huge improvement on the system of scrolls. And the industry of copying these out by hand occupied a whole class of literate workers called copyists. In many book production centres a reader would read a book sentence by sentence out loud, while as many as twenty or more scribes would write what was being said. Supervisors checked the pages later for accuracy. When they were done they had not one new copy of a book, but twenty, or more, depending on the number of scribes that could fit into the scriptorium. The mass production of books had arrived. Surely those working in this new system could not conceive of any better method of making books than what they had at their disposal.

From scriptorium to printing press

But then a fellow named Gutenberg, about a thousand years later, realised just how tedious this process was. And it was also open to too many variations in the books as each scribe's work was likely to be slightly different. He worked out a new system whereby individual letters could be attached to a plate, the plate covered (often with a brush) by ink, and new pages stamped until the ink needed to be reapplied. Making a plate for each page of a book took quite some time. But once the plates were set (a process called typesetting), hundreds and even thousands of identical copies of a book could be produced. The cost of books came down dramatically with the invention of the printing press. In the late medieval period, few could conceive that any better method of making books could be found.

The emergence of modern printing

Of course, many refinements were made to the printing press, and the tedious job of hand setting the letters was largely replaced in most presses by the twentieth-century. By late in the twentieth century, printing presses, and typesetting, was being linked to computer programs. But it still took time (often two to three hours) to set up the press for a print run, and it was inefficient to do small runs of books because of the time needed to get the press ready for the next job. By the early twenty-first century print-on-demand (POD) meant that a small number of copies could be produced, and the machine could quickly go on to the next print order.

e-books and the predicted demise of the traditional book.

The next innovation was truly revolutionary. It was the idea that books did not need to be printed at all. They could be stored electronically and read from a screen. It is one of the most radical revolutions in books in the last three thousand years. As noted earlier, e-books have not, so far, been as quick to displace the existing system as many at first thought.

So why do traditional books remain so popular? It is difficult, if not impossible, to lend an e-book to a friend, and every time you change or upgrade your e-reader, you will likely lose your e-library. And there is also something special about the feel of a real book in the hand. You can take a hard copy book anywhere and not worry about its battery life, and many find hard copy easier on the eyes. Others simply prefer the weight and feel of an actual book when they board a bus, train or plane, when they recline on a deck chair or hammock on holiday, or when they sit down on a familiar armchair in the evening. Perhaps for some of these reasons, e-books are not replacing hard copy books as predicted, and may never do so, despite their many obvious benefits.

Booksellers and libraries

The selling and collecting of books go hand in hand with their writing and production. In the famous House of Wisdom that existed in Baghdad under the Abbasids, books were not only copied, but a series of bookstores and a great library were also part of the complex. In late medieval Europe, when the printing press was developed, booksellers quickly sprang up in connection with each press, to sell their wares. Regardless of the form that books might take, readers will continue to buy them. And certain individuals and organisations will continue to collect and store them. The history of the bookseller and the library is as old as books themselves, and will continue as long as books are being written and published, in whatever form.

And books will likely continue on for some time in a form similar to what they are now. But even if they do not, we must remember that stories transcend books, and will survive any transformation in either the form of books themselves, or the way in which they are sold and stored. While writers have moved from stylus to quill, to pen, to typewriter, to personal computer and finally to laptop or notepad, the creative process involved in composing books has changed very little. There will always be a place for the creators and tellers of new stories, in whatever form these are produced and enjoyed.

Writers should not worry about the future of books. Books will exist as long as there are storytellers, and storytellers will exist as long as there are people to hear them.

Exercise: Literary field trip

You might want to find a writing or book-loving friend to take with you on this exercise. Using the internet, find all of the following in your regional centre, suburb, or city: general bookstores, second-hand bookstores, Christian bookstores, public libraries, university or other educational libraries, quality church libraries. Visit each one. Familiarise yourself with what they have to offer. You are much more likely to make use of these resources in future once you know they exist, where they are located, and what you might find in them.

Postscript:

The Sacred Life of Words

> *'In the beginning was the Word, and the Word was with God, and the Word was God ... And the Word became flesh and lived among us.'*
>
> – St. John the Evangelist

There is something sacred about words. This is especially true from the perspective of the Christian tradition. We confess Jesus as God incarnate to be 'the Word made flesh' (John 1); God's word is celebrated using the device of an elaborate alphabet poem (Psalm 119), Jesus is called the 'logos' or word, and he speaks to us the 'words of life' (John 6:68).

The very first book of the Bible tells us that human beings are made in God's image (Genesis 1:27). We reflect this image in many ways. One of these is certainly our ability to communicate with God and with one another using words.

Christianity, like Judaism before it, is a religion of the book. While other ancient faiths made images of their gods, the God of Abraham, Isaac and Jacob, the God and Father of Jesus Christ, chose to reveal himself and to be revealed in words. And these words were written down in books. When the Romans wanted to punish the followers of a particular religion, they destroyed their shrines. When the Roman emperor Diocletian sought to destroy Christianity, he tried to destroy all the copies of their sacred writings. Even the enemies of this new faith recognised that it was a faith founded upon words – words written down in books.

The good news of Jesus, the Word made flesh, is given to us in written, human words. Because of this focus on God's word given to us in written words, literacy spread with the expansion of Christianity as people learned to read specifically so they could read the words of the Bible.

Christian communities, founded upon the words of scripture, also made rich use of words in their liturgies, their songs and their prayers. God speaks to us in words, and we respond in worship and praise in words. We confess our faith in words. It is words that contain, describe and record our stories, our hopes, our histories. The Christian faith has been thoroughly embedded not only in the Word, but in words. The legacy has been a tradition steeped not only in the appreciation of its sacred writings, but of literature in general.

This is the tradition inherited by the Christian writer. Words are the tools of our craft. But we know that words are more than just functional tools we use to organise our relationships and societies. Words are sacred, and those who work with words, who craft and shape them, participate in something sacred. The words we write take on their own life, their own sacred life. Words work their way into the minds and hearts of readers to inspire, challenge, encourage and transform.

Words are symbol-bearers. They convey and represent so much more than a collection of sounds or bits of information. Collectively, words are the audible, and when written, the visible image of truths which transcend their individual sounds and meanings. There is something sacramental about words. They point to and participate in a reality greater than themselves. And when they point to the love and grace of God in Jesus Christ, they fulfil their highest calling.

The act of writing, whether of novels, poems, letters or other texts, is a sacred vocation. All who participate in this calling participate in the sacred life of words. We participate in the life of God, the Word made flesh, who came and dwelt among us.

ACKNOWLEDGEMENTS

In the years I have spent teaching creative writing, speaking at writing seminars, and working on various sections of this manuscript, I have accumulated a great indebtedness to many students, readers and friends. Mentioning everyone who provided an insight, pointed out an unclear sentence, asked a good question or suggested an addition would be an impossible task, even if I had been keeping a list. But some I can mention.

Firstly, many thanks to the several groups of students at Tabor Adelaide from 2005 to 2010 to whom I taught Creative Writing, and for whom earlier versions of this manuscript served as a text. I would also like to thank my colleagues in the creative writing department at Tabor from those days, from whom I learned much, especially Rosanne Hawke, Claire Bell, Yr Ham, Ben Morton and James Cooper.

Also, I acknowledge with gratitude the much help and support I received from the members of the writing group to which I belong, Literati. I have learned much from them over the past fifteen years. Special thanks to Literati members Valerie Volk and Caz Williams who read the manuscript and provided numerous suggestions for improvement.

I would also like to thank my editor at Morning Star Publishing, Amanda McKenna, for her enthusiastic support throughout the process, and Nola Passmore of The Write Flourish, a former student and now professional editor, for the very thorough, professional and insightful copyediting of the manuscript.

All of these and many others have played a big role in making this book possible.

Mark Worthing

www.ingramcontent.com/pod-product-compliance
Lightning Source LLC
Chambersburg PA
CBHW070032100426
42740CB00013B/2668

9780647530474